WRESTLING THE WORLD

WRESTLING THE WORLD
THE LIFE AND TIMES OF
WORLD RODEO CHAMPION JACK RODDY

KATIE COONEY

An authorized biography.

Copyright © 2019 by Katie Cooney

Jacket design by Katie Cooney.
Book cover image: John and Jack Roddy.

If you would like permission to use material from the book (other than reviewing), please contact the author. Thank you for your support of the author and subject.

www.katiecooney.com
www.jackroddy.com

First Edition: December 2019

Library of Congress Number: 2019910563
ISBNs: 978-1-7333558-0-3 (paperback) and
ISBN: 978-1-7333558-1-0 (ebook)

This book is lovingly dedicated to my mother,
Ruthie Traub Devore,
whose endless and steadfast love, support and encouragement
made me who I am.

Table of Contents

Introduction by Monty Roberts	13
Introduction by Chris Cox	15
The American Cowboy & Rodeo History	17
Steer Wrestling	19
About the Man	21
Chapter 1	25
Chapter 2	31
Chapter 3	45
Chapter 4	77
Chapter 5	83
Chapter 6	101
Chapter 7	123
Chapter 8	139
Chapter 9	151
Chapter 10	167
Chapter 11	195
Chapter 12	213
Chapter 13	225
Chapter 14	233
Chapter 15	259
Chapter 16	265
Chapter 17	273
Chapter 18	285
Chapter 19	295
Chapter 20	301
First Place Rodeo Wins	313
Epilogue	315
Acknowledgements	317
Thank You's	318

WRESTLING THE WORLD

Wrestling the World

Introduction by Monty Roberts
Rodeo Champion, The Man Who Listens to Horses, Author and Flag Is Up Farms

To write the introduction of Jack Roddy's biography is a very difficult task indeed. One must be informed the man is a first-generation US citizen with his father hailing from Ireland. Jack's dad, John, was a brilliant businessman. Like the perfect Irish businessman, he started a collection of bars.

Roddy's Bars and the Boots n' Saddle are what John Roddy called his bars. They were in San Francisco and San Jose and immediately attracted the attention of the far west cowboys who enjoyed their evenings in typical cowboy saloons. Jack, born in 1937 became the provider of rodeo competition trophies and photographs that added flavor to the bars decor.

I became acquainted with the Roddy family through a horse called Chongo, who carried Jack to his early championship trophy saddles and awards throughout the US

Katie Cooney

and Canada.

Jack Roddy is a friend of virtually everyone I know in the rodeo world. Saloons to a golf course and a golf course to a cattle operation, Jack is all things Western, as well as a high-level businessman. The only anomaly I can remember about Jack Roddy is that he had a propensity, when he was young, for sleepwalking.

John W. Jones Sr., Allan Keller and I experienced Jack walking, talking and acting as though he was awake when actually he was sound asleep. Jack Roddy became lasting friends with those of every persuasion throughout his life.

I await with great anticipation to read each word Jack has chosen to include in his biography. He is a special man who captured my attention at every segment of life. From junior rodeos through Cal Poly University to world championships and as a member of the Professional Rodeo Cowboys Association board, Jack has garnered the admiration of all.

Introduction by Chris Cox
Rodeo Champion, Chris Cox Horsemanship Company and Diamond Double C Ranch

Jack Roddy is a Legend not only in the Rodeo World, but in the western industry.

Jack and my dad were students at Cal Poly in the late 1950s and dated the same women. My father told me stories about Jack throughout my childhood in Australia.

He represents the cowboy with honor and integrity. Always well dressed in public with a pressed shirt and hat. Our trips to Ireland and Australia provide memories that will be talked about for years.

Jack and Donna are not only friends, but family.

There is no better entertainment than listening to Jack share stories of his life, as he sips on a Scotch and soda.

With countless awards and Hall of Fame inductions, he always takes time to talk to fans, including our youth.

Katie Cooney

Jack has inspired and mentored many world champions that today are household names in the rodeo business.

His character and giving personality are a dying breed in today's world. It's an honor to call him my mentor, friend, and family.

The American Cowboy & Rodeo History

Cowboy legend is perhaps the greatest story of the American West. A vision of weathered men on horseback driving cattle across the dusty plains of Kansas, Oklahoma, and Texas describes the cowboys of lore. He grew up working the land, his very soul formed from dirt, sweat and adversity. The American cowboy is a global icon, stoic, strong and steely-eyed. The cowboy is a maverick, a man who knows his true north and rides for the brand. Film legend, John Wayne, embodied the essence of the cowboy, with his swagger, confidence and no-nonsense manner. Countless boys dreamed of being a cowboy and for some that dream came true.

Rodeos date back to the late 1800s. When the first Anglo-Americans settled in Texas and they blended with the Spanish-American cultures. Vaqueros cultivated roping, riding, herding and branding and taught the Anglos, who were later called cowboys. With the introduction of fences, range cowboys now had boundaries. Small and large ranches alike came together for festivities and cowboys got a chance to show off their skills in bronc riding and roping skills. Annual contests were soon established.

Seasonal cowboys took work in wild-west shows made famous by William F. Cody (Buffalo Bill). Cody's first exhibition was on the 4th of July 1882 in North Platte, Nebraska. He took the show on the road throughout the United States, Great Britain and Europe.

In 1883, the rodeo in Pecos, Texas issued the first prize money and in 1888 the rodeo in Prescott, Arizona first charged admission. The public mostly viewed rodeoing as entertainment, not a sport. In 1929, the Rodeo Association of America (RAA) was created by rodeo producers to legitimize the sport. RAA set standards and fair practices, monitored judges, created titles and the point system. Although, the RAA legitimized the sport, the producers were making the majority of the money, not the cowboys.

In 1936, 61 cowboys voted to strike after seeing the prize money offered at the rodeo in Boston. The producers decided to give them a better cut of the profit. Empowered, the cowboys formed the Cowboys Turtle Association (CTA) on November 6, 1939. The purpose of the new CTA was to improve earnings, improve fairness in judging and the cowboys' image. In 1945, the CTA reorganized and became the Rodeo Cowboys Association (RCA). In 1975, the RCA became the Professional Rodeo Cowboys Association (PRCA). The PRCA brought events into line and standardized rules. Saddle-bronc riding, bareback riding, bull riding, calf roping, steer wrestling team roping, and single steer roping were now sanctioned rodeo events. Barrel racing is the only cowgirl event at standard PRCA rodeos. Cowboys and cowgirls compete in timed or judged events. Over the season, each dollar won equates to one point; total points determine the world champions at the end of the year at the National Finals Rodeo (NFR).

The RCA grew to 3,200 members in 1966. More than 600 rodeos were produced in the United States and Canada, with crowds in the tens of thousands and cash purses totaling more than one million. The best cowboys in their events were making $30,000 dollars a season. Today, that's an estimated $223,000.

Steer Wrestling

Steer wrestling means jumping from a running horse onto the horns of a 700-pound steer at 30 miles per hour or better, bringing the animal to a stop and twisting it to the ground.

Bulldogging was introduced to rodeo in 1907 by Bill Pickett, a black Texas cowboy nicknamed "the Dusky Demon." "Dogging," or steer wrestling as it is now called, went on to become a regular and popular rodeo event, though it's never been a part of working ranch life.

The steer wrestler has a horseback partner called a "hazer" to help him. When the steer bursts from the chute, it trips a barrier line which drops and allows the wrestler and hazer to take off in hot pursuit. The hazer keeps the steer running in a straight line as the bulldogger leans from his speeding horse to get a solid grip on the steer's horns. He transfers his weight to the steer, lifts his boots from the stirrups and digs his heels into the dirt to stop the steer and throw it to the ground. The steer is considered down when it's lying flat, with its head and all four feet pointing in the same direction. If the steer gets loose, the bulldogger may take only one step to catch him. As in all timed events, the cowboy is assessed a 10-second penalty if he breaks the barrier line. A top steer wrestler may dog his steer in five seconds or less.

Katie Cooney

Wrestling the World

About the Man

Kick back, grab yourself a toddy,
We'll talk about Jack Roddy.

It may not be the place and time,
But try to get a name like that to rhyme.

He should have been called Cowboy, 'cause that's what he is,
And he has two buckles that are only his.

He went down the road, not to crack a whip,
But to win a championship.

Some say he left with not more than a blessin',
And when he came back, he'd won the steer wrestlin'.

'66 and '68 were his years to rule,
He'd left the other doggers in a drool.

He's a straight and he's lean as he is in life,
Which give me a good place to mention his wife.

But this is for Jack, so Donna we won't mention your glory,
For that, rodeo fans, is another story.

You can ride with this man and gather his cattle,
But when ya do…"take a deep seat in your saddle."

Katie Cooney

He's the general with unpolished brass,
But miss a hole and he'll chew your ass,
Then in the same breath ask,
"Don't you think they'll love this grass?"

If you want to avoid his awful retort,
Just ride Brown's Canyon on the Bettencourt.

I apologize for the referral to the burro and don't want to offend,
So I guess this story should end.

By Dennis Broderick

Wrestling the World

'All I ever wanted to be was a cowboy.'
— Jack Roddy

Katie Cooney

Chapter 1

'With a fourth-grade education, he became head of the family.'
- Jack Roddy

Heroes overcome long odds. Focus, courage and daring allow mere mortals to capitalize on pivotal moments that shape their destiny and become legends. Their stories inspire and lend bravery. Two-time world rodeo champion Jack Roddy is one of those legends. He never gave up and he reached the top, from origins that are the essence of the American dream.

The Roddy story began far from the American West, in a small village called Ballaghaderreen in the county of Roscommon, Ireland. In 1905, Jack's father John was born in a dirt floor, thatch-roof farmhouse with stone walls three feet thick. John was the second-born son to Winifred and Michael, a farming family of modest means.

Life in Ireland was tough. When blight started killing the potato crop in 1845, the Great Famine began. A million people starved and another million emigrated, reducing the population by 25 percent. Those that stayed behind farmed the land to feed their children and struggled to pay rent to British landlords.

Roddy owned a 40-acre farm, a few dairy cows and a small but productive garden. The family fetched water from a well 200 feet from the house. A wall separated the pigs and cattle from the home. The livestock and garden gave the family an edge on starvation and once the cows birthed, Father Michael sold them at market. The Roddys were better off than most.

Michael was the first to farm with a horse in the village. Son John's love of horses began in the field, where the children worked when not in school. It was a hard life, but there were good times too.

The Roddy clan quickly grew to five children, spreading their income thin. First born son Patrick died of unknown causes in May 1915 at age 10. With his death, John became the eldest child. Life in Ireland was unbearable with malnourished children, the spread of tuberculosis, and a dire economic outlook. Michael joined the cast of desperate thousands sailing across the Atlantic to find work in America. In fetid, rat infested ships they made their way to New York harbor. For Michael, this was the chance to ensure his family's survival.

Arriving in New York City in 1915, Roddy saw business-window signs and want ads that made it clear: "N.I.N.A."— No Irish Need Apply. Undeterred, he secured work in the far-off copper mines of Butte, Montana where Irish were tolerated.

Butte was nicknamed the Richest Hill on Earth: Its underbelly was loaded with copper. The Copper Kings, industrialists William Andrews Clark, Marcus Daly and F. Augustus Heinze battled over the control of the mines for over 30 years. Copper was key in the burgeoning production of telephones, electric lights and the telegraph. When demand peaked, the Butte mines produced one-third of the total copper supply in the United States. From 1892 to 1903, $300 billion in copper was excavated. The Anaconda mine was the top producer.

By 1900, Butte had more Irish immigrants than any other city in the country. In 1916, 14,500 Irish miners worked the mines in the isolated and polluted town. The creek turned brown from sewage and the smelting of copper. Locals called the creek "Copper Creek". The barren landscape only emphasized the cruel work and hard living of the miners and their families.

Miners worked rotating shifts around the clock, 365 days a year. Newly arrived, unskilled immigrants like Roddy drew the most treacherous assignments. Deaths were common from unstable rock collapsing or fire. Paychecks were high, but so were the risks. Between 1880 and 1920, more than 2,000 miners lost their lives to accidents and occupational disease working underground. From 1880 until at least 1915, mining industrialists considered workers an expendable commodity and regarded accidents, disease and disabilities as the cost of doing business, according to research at Montana State University by Brian Lee Shovers. If a miner survived to

Wrestling the World

40 years old, he was considered not only old, but lucky. For most it was just a matter of time before an injury or death.

The Granite Mountain Mine Disaster in 1917, still regarded as one of the worst hard-rock mine accidents in the nation's history claimed 168 miners one night. A spark accidentally touched off a fire that ripped through the shafts. Miners also died from carbon monoxide and steam from efforts to extinguish the fire.

Roddy most likely worked for the Anaconda Copper Mining Company, known simply as "The Company" by 1914. The Company had full control over the mines, the town and most of the Montana government.

With the onset of World War I, demand for copper grew and Irish miners worried they'd be drafted. The mood in Butte was tense. Irish miners detested thinking they'd join forces and fight alongside the British.

Roddy's concern of being drafted died with him, just as the war began in 1918. A fiery explosion in the belly of the hill took his life. On January 29, 1918, at age 43, Michael Roddy became another number in the Butte death registry.

Word of Michael's death reached Ballaghaderreen. Fate kicked into motion for elder son John. At 13 years old, with a fourth-grade education, he became head of the family. He reluctantly quit school and began working the farm. That was the end of his schooling.

A life of endless chores became routine for John. Younger siblings Marian, 12, James, 9, Helena, 8 and young Michael helped tend the 40-acre farm when not in school. Mother and son tilled the fields, milked the cows, churned the butter and tended the chickens and pigs.

Michael's brother in San Francisco mailed books to the children, depicting the American West in Cowboy-and-Indian stories of adventure and daring.

Uncle Roddy wrote letters describing adventures on his ranch outside of San Francisco, where he had horses and cattle. Through the long days of work, John dreamed of the ranch, hoping to see that magical land.

Katie Cooney

Years passed on the farm. By eighteen years old, John stood 6 feet 1 inch tall. And no matter how hard he worked, no matter how hard he tried, he only had a fourth-grade education and no opportunities in hand. There was no future for him in Ireland, he had to leave. John saved for passage to New York. He'd get to California and work on his uncle's ranch and send money home like his father did.

On June 6, 1926, John boarded the S.S. Scythia and set sail from Cobh, known today as Queenstown, Ireland, for the United States. The ship's manifest listed John as 21 years old, a single laborer who could speak English, with a mother in the County Roscommon, the city of Ballaghaderreen. His destination was listed as Philadelphia, where his aunt resided.

Ten days later, the ship entered New York Harbor. He passed the health inspection on Ellis Island and moved to immigration. He presented his visa, No. 20665—issued in Dublin. He bought a train ticket to Philadelphia and had $18 to spare.

John arrived in Philadelphia and found a job as a landscaper. For 18 months he worked, saved and sent money home.

At age 23, he boarded a train west for San Francisco and for the ranch he'd imagined. He left Philadelphia riding on a dream.

After he arrived, John and his uncle headed to the ranch in Marin County. On arrival, John saw nothing but a barren, 20-acre potato patch overlooking San Francisco. Later, he walked to the edge of the Marin Headlands and felt the bitter smite of consuming disappointment. The potato patch held no promise for him. His dreams of cowboys, horses and cattle, were quickly swallowed by the rolling fog cascading in from the Pacific.

Heavy-hearted, but no time for self-pity, John looked for work. Little did he know, his future success lay across the bay in San Francisco.

SS Scythia Passenger List June 6th, 1926. Roddy #12.

Katie Cooney

SS Scythia.

Chapter 2

'There's no such word as can't.'
— John Roddy

Irish Catholics had a tight grip on San Francisco during the first part of the 20th century. They held powerful leadership in city government, the police force, fire department and the church.

John left the ranch in Marin and headed for the city. He tried out for the fire department with high expectations; Irish firemen were respected and well-paid. But he didn't make the cut. He saw few other choices for good employment. His street smarts and determination were keen, but he had only a fourth-grade education.

The Volstead Act, or Prohibition, continued to ban the manufacturing, sale and transportation of liquor under the 18th Amendment. But in cities like San Francisco, the powers could and would turn a blind eye to bootlegging.

Politicians, well-to-do citizens and heiresses stockpiled their own libations to be enjoyed at lavish parties and private dinner gatherings behind closed doors, far from the snooping eyes of Temperance teetotalers.

In less lofty circles, alcohol was being made in old bathtubs and other makeshift equipment to keep up with the demand of ordinary folk, coast to coast. As Progressive Movement members tried to cure some of society's ills by banning alcohol, budding entrepreneurs discovered an insatiable national thirst, they got busy meeting that demand. The nation was awash in high times and high hopes; it was a time of opportunity.

Katie Cooney

Prohibition was meant to rid society of its ills caused by alcohol, but once instituted, it created a host of new problems. Authorities lost all control of alcohol manufacturing and distribution. Speakeasies and "private clubs" replaced saloons, bad liquor began poisoning and killing people, crime increased, and people were drinking more alcohol than ever before. The production, sale and transportation of alcohol went from legal businesses into the opportunistic hands of criminals, small-time entrepreneurs and the iron clad fist of the mob, which would extend its grasp into crime, politics and law enforcement nationwide.

When the opportunity arose to work for an Irish bootlegging operation in San Francisco, John took it. John worked side-by-side with Irish immigrants like himself in a hidden operation in San Francisco's Dogpatch area, a gritty neighborhood along the waterfront, east of Potrero Hill. Late one night, one of the workers rushed in and screamed the police were on the way. The men grabbed their gear and ran. John kept making moonshine.

Hours passed and John continued to stand over the still. If he was discovered, he'd likely go to jail. The consequences were real, but he saw few options.

Later, the bootleggers returned and found John still at work. They moved to resume their places, but John told them they were done. They had run; he had stayed. An argument ensued. John told them to get lost and took over the operation.

Staying with the still paid off. He was now in business. Not exactly the cowboy he'd dreamed of, but he was a maverick charting his own course.

Growing up poor had taught John to improvise. One of his stills operated on the third floor of an apartment building. Lugging alcohol and materials up and down three flights of stairs took time and exposed the operation to prying residents. Runners also risked dropping the glass bottles full of new liquor on the stairs and in the hallway. John found a better solution: He ran the whiskey through a garden hose out an apartment window facing the street. Down three flights, the booze drained into barrels stashed in the trunks of cars at the curb. No muss, no fuss, no stairway.

The Wall Street Crash of 1929 stopped the country in its tracks. Wealthy socialites suddenly found themselves broke. The banks were going bust. The post-war party was over. The Great Depression would weigh heavily on the next decade. As America reeled, John kept making alcohol.

The alcohol made and sold on the black market created its own economy, without the burden of taxation. If Prohibition was overturned, the federal government and the people would benefit; taxes from alcohol sales would flow to state and local governments that desperately needed the money.

State conventions and rallies called for an end to Prohibition. Politicians railed, editors fulminated, and Congress supported repeal. President Franklin Roosevelt signed the 21st Amendment to the Constitution, repealing Prohibition in December 1933. The amendment was the first and only one to ratify an earlier amendment, the 18th.

John had lived and worked in the rough, raw streets of San Francisco known as the Barbary Coast, on Pacific Avenue between Montgomery and Stockton streets. He knew the blue-collar workers and poor immigrants who lived in the neighborhood. Like him, they'd come to America poor and eager for a better life.

After repeal, John took his savings and bought a 12-stool bar at 3rd and Mission in the South of Market neighborhood. The area was literally on the wrong side of the tracks: It had been known as "South of the Slot," after the cable-car slots along the Market Street thoroughfare.

John was a legitimate businessman now. It was a working-class bar, but John insisted his bartenders wear a uniform of white shirts, black ties and slacks. They kept the bar spotless. John was meticulous about cleaning and kept everything in strict order, from the bottles lined up behind the bar to the wood floor. One unbreakable rule at Roddy's Bar at 3rd and Mission: No fighting, so people could relax and enjoy a drink.

The Port of San Francisco was a popular place for sailors on shore leave. They disembarked their ships and headed straight for the bars. Once oiled up, they were easy targets for pickpockets, thieves and dishonest bartenders. Sometimes their drinks were drugged—they got "slipped a Mickey"—and they were rolled and robbed. Hung over sailors awoke to find they'd been cleaned out of cash and anything else that could be fenced, pawned or sold.

Roddy's Bar had high standards, despite its spot in the tough part of the city.

Other bars might take advantage of drunken sailors, but at Roddy's, the bartenders took the drunken sailors' money, put it in the safe with their name on it and put a note in their pocket saying, "Your money's at Roddy's Bar; come get it."

Sailors spread the word that Roddy's was a place you could trust. The white shirts, cleanliness, no-fighting and no-stealing rules stood out from other joints. He built a reputation on hard work, honesty, integrity and a bit of polish.

Once the 12-stool bar was breaking even, John saved for his next acquisition, a neighborhood liquor store. Shortly after buying the store, he opened another bar he also called Roddy's, four blocks away at 7th and Mission. John felt a sense of security. The bars and liquor store were doing well.

In the summer of 1934, the International Longshoremen's Association, or ILA, renewed its efforts to establish a presence on the West Coast. Longshoremen banded together for better pay and working conditions. The West Coast Longshoremen's Strike, led by Australian-born sailor and American union leader Harry Bridges, lasted 83 days.

The longshoremen walked out May 9 and the bosses hired scabs and strikebreakers to take their places. After a two-month strike, city police broke through the picket lines and violence erupted. Two men died and 70 were injured in the ensuing riots. Governor Frank Merriam sent in the National Guard to bring order.

In support of the strike, 100,000 other union workers walked off their jobs. The general strike lasted four days. Citizens saw tanks rolling down the streets and uniformed men with weapons policing the intersections. It appeared a revolution was in the works. Finally, shipowners and the longshoremen agreed to resume negotiating and made a deal, though labor troubles continued between the bosses and unions, and the unions themselves.

Roddy's loyal customers were the longshoremen and union workers. They were having a tough time making ends meet and John decided he'd extend credit to the longshoremen who'd joined the strike. He knew it was risky, but it was either extend the credit or have no business at all. John knew the strike wouldn't last forever and sympathized with the strikers. His father had been killed working for the bosses and he knew the back-breaking labor the longshoremen did and the physical risk they faced.

When the strike ended, Roddy's bars sat empty. Business dried up and John got wind the longshoremen were drinking at other bars in the neighborhood. He realized the men couldn't pay their IOUs and were staying away. So, John spread the word there would be a big event in front of Roddy's at 3rd and Mission on Friday—the longshoremen's payday. Everyone was welcome.

Friday at 5:30 p.m., local longshoremen, other union men and neighborhood regulars gathered in front of Roddy's anticipating a show. John opened the door of the 12-stool bar. Like soldiers marching into battle, he and the bartenders carried wooden crates containing the last three months' IOUs.

One by one they dumped the contents of the crates into a pile. There was no mistaking the slips of paper. Scribbled by hand, each note contained the type of alcohol consumed, how much, the name of the patron and the promise of payment.

John looked around the crowd, then doused the IOUs with gasoline. He dramatically struck a match and threw it in. The IOUs burned to ash.

Decades later, John recalled the story to Jack. He advised him: Don't ever take credit.

As the bars returned to life, John took an interest in a young woman named Ann Byrnes. Her mother was American-born Irish, her father, a native of Ireland. Her maiden name used the Irish spelling for Burns, but due to racial prejudices against the Irish, she changed it to the Scottish spelling—Byrnes. She worked as a secretary in the city.

Ann's father had joined the Irish Republican Army as a youth and became a captain. Mr. Burns nurtured a deep hatred of the British and supported the Irish Republican

Army with money to buy weapons. A carpenter by trade, he'd built many homes in the Richmond District of San Francisco. He'd invested heavily in the stock market and lost everything in the 1929 crash. As an older man, he went back to carpentry work wearing a white shirt and tie.

In 1935, John and Ann married in San Francisco.

At family gatherings, John teased his father-in-law, "you know Mr. Burns, you know Britain needed to have a little part of Ireland." Mr. Burns turned scarlet with rage and pounded the table in protest. The turkey jumped six inches off the table. John then turned and gave a wink to his bride.

John looked again to expand. Bradley's 5 & 10, a gay bar in the Fillmore District, was struggling to stay in business. The owners couldn't seem to establish a loyal clientele. Bradley's claimed to be the "longest bar in the world," spanning a city block between Geary and Post. In addition, it boasted "the tallest and shortest bartenders in the world," Hank stretching 7 feet, 8 inches and Terry at 4 feet, 11 inches. This was an opportunity and John jumped at it.

In 1937, Bradley's 5 & 10 became Roddy's Fish Bowl. It took a while to gain traction. John and Ann brainstormed for ideas that would entice locals and tourists alike. Ann suggested a 14-ounce beer glass with the bar's logo on it, costing a nickel. Customers loved the huge glass of beer and tourists enjoyed a souvenir from "the longest bar in the world." The 14-ounce glass, the world-record longest bar and the tallest and shortest bartenders lit a spark. The bar thrived as a tourist attraction and a local hangout. Seven bartenders, each shift, hustled to keep up with the demand.

Clients challenged John's claim of "longest bar in the world," and he vowed to substantiate the claim. He hired two men to measure a bar in New York City and one in China that made the same claim. The men returned, and reported Roddy's Fish Bowl was the longest bar in the world—by five inches. John had won by a horse's neck. He concocted a "By A Horse's Neck" cocktail to celebrate.

The bars ran smoothly, by the rules; cleanliness, white shirts & ties, no fights and workers who didn't swear or steal. John hired a bar-spotting service, determined to maintain his standards. The spotters reported on customer service, bartenders, drink pouring and behavior. If the bartenders cursed or swore, they were fired. If they were sloppy or didn't wear the customary white shirt and black tie, they were fired.

Every Monday, Acme Brewing company's horse drawn wagons pulled up and delivered a load of 31-gallon wooden kegs full of beer—450 kegs every month. That's nearly 128,000 14-ounce beers.

In 1937, the Golden Gate Bridge opened in May after five years of construction. Spanning the mouth of the bay from Marin County to the Presidio, the three-mile engineering wonder was called the most beautiful bridge in the world. Celebrations lasted a week and more. Before the bridge opened to automobiles, pedestrians could walk the span. Locals and tourists crowded the bridge with their sweethearts, families and children.

John joined the San Mateo Horse Posse years before and that day, he and 56 fellow San Mateo Horse Posse members rode back and forth across the bridge, then rode on downtown and crossed Market Street as the crowd cheered. The men headed straight for Roddy's Fish Bowl. Men and women crowded the bar celebrating, drinking and singing as 56 men entered on horseback.

Lore has it that if just one more horse had entered the floor would have collapsed. Luckily, the horses only tore up the carpeted floors and no one was hurt.

Fifty-six horses lined the bar. It set a world record for the number of long faces in a happy bar.

Katie Cooney

John Roddy in 1933.

Roddy's Fish Bowl, formerly Bradley's 5 and 10, San Francisco.

Roddy's Fish Bowl ashtray.

Roddy's Fish Bowl matchbook.

Roddy's Fish Bowl bartender with nickel beers.

San Mateo Horse Posse.

John Roddy, San Mateo Horse Posse member.

John Roddy left showing horse.

Ann and John Roddy riding in Golden Gate Park, San Francisco.

Katie Cooney

John Roddy center on ship traveling to Ireland.

Chapter 3

'They always remember a king. They never remember a bum.'

John Thomas "Jack" Roddy was born October 3, 1937 in San Francisco. Family members, longshoremen and tourists toasted Jack's birth at the Roddy bars. The Roddy clan in Ireland celebrated over pints at the pub in Ballaghaderreen. Ann and John brought Jack home to 121 Entrada Court, in San Francisco's Ingleside Terraces neighborhood.

In 1939, as the bars and liquor stores turned a profit, John bought a rodeo grounds in Colma, just south of San Francisco and began producing rodeos. John met Charlie Maggini at one of his rodeos and struck up a fast friendship. They shared a love of the West and Maggini was the 1929 World Champion in team and steer roping. He was the first cowboy to win two world championships in a single year. Maggini mentored ropers, sharing his skills with the next generation of rodeo cowboys.

"Charlie's the guy who got my family involved in rodeo," Jack remembered. "He rode horses for my dad and showed the first winner of the reined cow-horse class at the Cow Palace…a horse by the name of Johnny, in 1942."

"Maggini was the best cowboy I'd ever seen. He learned from the Mexican vaqueros how to train the California bridle horse. He rode saddle-broncs, bulls, roped calves, team roped, steer roped and trained some of the top bridle horses. I used to go to brandings with him. He's the best hand in a branding corral that I've ever seen, bar none. Will Rogers came out here to California to rope with Maggini; he'd heard Maggini was an artist with a rope. He was a cowboy all the way. Maggini was still breaking horses just before he died," in 1982.

John bought Jack a horse called Midgy when Jack was three. John, Maggini and Jack rode through Golden Gate Park on Saturdays and Maggini instilled in Jack his deep knowledge and understanding of horses. When Jack wasn't riding Midgy at rodeo events, he sat atop Maggini's shoulders watching the events.

Maggini was also a skilled prankster. Jack learned to love this craft too.

John got deeply involved with the local rodeo community. In 1939, John and Bill Cresta, of Cresta Auto Parts, bankrolled the Golden Gate International Exposition Rodeo on Treasure Island. The exposition ran May 12-21, celebrating the building of the Golden Gate and Bay bridges, which had opened in 1936 and 1937.

Jack was diagnosed with severe asthma at five. He struggled to breathe in his early years. The doctor suggested the family move to a drier climate that summer. "As the fog nestled in, my lungs would begin to swell and I could hardly breathe," Jack recalled.

John searched for a summer home south of the city. He bought a 1,000-acre ranch on Sierra Road in the Alum Rock foothills of East San Jose and resettled the family.

John stocked the ranch with cattle, horses, chickens and ducks, and Jack thrived, watching his father and friends practice riding and roping in the arena.

In 1946, the family moved permanently to the ranch. John commuted from San Jose to San Francisco to manage the bars, liquor stores and the arena in Colma. The family embraced the country life. Jack grew healthy and strong.

Success came early. At age 8, Jack won first in a horse show. He'd shown his family's bridle horses at the Gilroy Rodeo and took home his first winner's belt buckle.

John needed help on the ranch while he was at work in town. He hired friend and fellow Irishman Ike Chisholm, a steelworker and a butcher in "Butchertown", in the South San Francisco stockyards.

On hot summer days, Jack entertained himself riding horses, roping and playing practical jokes. One day, he found Chisholm loading a recent shipment of hay into the barn. Sweat had soaked Chisholm as he bucked each bale and packed it into the barn.

In the hot dusty sunlight, Jack tossed stones at Chisholm. Chisholm tried to catch him, but Jack darted away. He returned and started tossing stones again. Chisholm lost patience and waited inside until Jack ran back up to the barn door. Chisholm sprang and caught him. Jack cried, kicked and pleaded to be let go, but Chisholm hoisted Jack up by his suspenders and hung him from a hay hook. Jack yelled for help, but everyone had gone to town. Chisholm resumed stacking hay.

John arrived a couple of hours later, heard Jack screaming for help and found him dangling from the hook. John turned and found Chisholm.

"Hey Chisholm, what's me boy doing hanging up there by his suspenders?" John asked.

"Your boy was throwing rocks at me and I hung him up there to dry," Chisholm replied.

John turned and unhooked Jack. Then he paddled him.

In 1947, John took Jack to Ballaghaderreen for a visit. Jack, 10, summered with his grandmother and cousins.

Mrs. Roddy lived in the same thatched cottage where John had grown up. It had no indoor plumbing and Jack was tasked with fetching water at the well behind the house. John offered to install a water pipe. Jack remembered his grandmother's response: "Yank, we've been fetching water for years and we'll continue fetching water for years."

John bought a Hillman Minx car to travel around the island. John left the car for the family. When he returned two years later, he found the car in the same spot. Family members preferred their bicycles. They'd been doing that for years, too.

At the end of their visit, family and friends threw a farewell party for John and Jack.

The neighboring Reagan sisters joined the festivities. Fiddles played, beer was drunk, and John told the Reagan sisters about the night he'd seen a group of banshees by the tree on the road. He told about the dread he'd felt since. The sisters recoiled in fear.

The party ended at 2 a.m. While Jack walked the Reagan sisters home, John and brother Michael ran out the back door, carrying large black raincoats toward the "banshee tree."

As Jack and the sisters neared the tree, John and Michael let loose mournful wailing and waved the raincoats over their heads. Jack and the sisters ran back to the Roddy house. The sisters spent the night.

Jack walked the sisters home in daylight. He'd known his father was behind the prank.

Father and son returned to San Jose at summer's end.

As Jack grew, he dreamed of a future in rodeo and cowboying.

John tried to discourage Jack from being a rodeo cowboy, but the more he spoke against it, the more Jack dug in. John decided to give Jack a taste of a real bucking horse and asked a friend to bring one to the ranch. The friend told Jack, "I brought this horse. Your dad wants to buy him for you." Jack remembered thinking, "Oh, boy. My dad's gonna buy me a rope horse."

Jack mounted ol' Bald Hornet. He went to rope a steer. The horse stopped short and went to bucking. Jack flew off and piled into the dirt, the wind knocked clear out of him.

The cowboys shouted for Jack to get back in the saddle. He ran Bald Hornet back down the arena and after the steer. Bald Hornet stopped short. Again, Jack raised a cloud of dust when he hit the ground.

One of the cowboys ran up and told him, "Jack, they're trying to kill you. Get those spurs off your boots!" Jack unbuckled the spurs and jumped back in the saddle. He took after the steer and roped it without a hitch.

"Okay, Bald Hornet, wanna mess with me?" Jack thought the next day. He cinched a bareback rig on him and took him to the bucking chute. He climbed aboard, opened the chute and Bald Hornet bucked him off. For a week, Jack tried to ride Bald Hornet. For a week, he got thrown.

But instead of turning Jack away from rodeoing, it intrigued him even more. Discouraged, John sold Bald Hornet to a rodeo. The horse had an illustrious career as a bucking horse.

When John decided to stay in the city a month and focus on his businesses, he put Jack in charge at the ranch.

Four gentle bulls were delivered before John's departure. John instructed Jack to be gentle with them—no fooling around.

When John left, Jack went to introduce himself to the bulls. Each was halter broke and wore a lead rope. Jack rode them before and after school. At first, Jack recalled, they were like "big fat old men." But they grew angrier with each ride and finally bucked Jack off. He rode those bulls every day for a month.

When John returned to the ranch his gentle bulls were "hot." John hadn't noticed the change right away, but when he approached them, they charged. He noticed the marks on their flanks, left by Jack's spurs. The truth became clear.

Despite the punishment that followed, Jack remembers the month fondly.

At 14, Jack entered his first Rodeo Cowboys Association rodeo, a Wild Horse Race in Gilroy, just south of San Jose. A team of three people—rider, shankman and muggler—work the race. The horse is let out of the chute and the shankman holds tight to the halter rope while the muggler steadies the horse by the head. The rider saddles and mounts the horse, then rides the bucking animal around the arena. Jack's team finished first, with him aboard the horse. He won $90. He loved it.

The following year, Jack competed at the Sheriff's Posse grounds at Alum Rock in

San Jose. He won the bareback competition and scored the All-Around title at age 15. "In those days, you could rodeo on a high school card. I always wanted to be a pro. Bill Linderman (a celebrated cowboy who won three world championships in 1950) signed my card," Jack said.

Jack enrolled in Bellarmine High School; a respected, private Jesuit boys' high school founded in 1851. His classmates included the sons of San Jose's most privileged and successful. Phillip and Dennis Crosby, the sons of entertainer and actor Bing Crosby, were in Jack's freshman class and son Gary was a senior at the time.

But the schooling sparked no interest in Jack. He wanted to be a cowboy. And his love of pranks didn't set well with the strict Jesuit brothers. He played pranks, skipped class and ended up in detention on Saturdays. Detention was called "jug" at the school.

"I spent more time in jug on Saturdays because I skipped school," Jack said. "Then I skipped jug. I never could get ahead."

Jack was kicked out of Bellarmine at the end of his freshman year. "I was just a problem child," he recalled. "I just wanted to ride and all that stuff."

John enrolled Jack in a San Jose public school called James Lick High School for his sophomore year.

Ann and John continued to discourage Jack from cowboying. That life was too hard, they said. He'd get hurt; he couldn't settle down; he'd make no money. John forbade Jack to pursue rodeos and tempers ran hot in the Roddy household. John and Jack were at constant odds. But Jack didn't care what his parents forbade. He wanted to be a cowboy.

And the shadow of his father's reputation loomed large. In San Francisco, Colma and San Jose, people knew him as "John Roddy's son." Jack was striving to become his own man, to make his own name. One day, he vowed, people would know John as "Jack Roddy's dad."

By 1952, John owned four bars between San Francisco and San Jose, two liquor stores in San Francisco, a rodeo arena in Colma, a home in San Francisco and the Sierra Ranch in San Jose. He commuted every day between San Jose and San Francisco. He worked tirelessly.

John felt Jack's work ethic needed strengthening. He enlisted a friend who owned a ranch in Denio, Nevada, to teach his son the value of hard labor. He told Jack that the friend needed help that summer breaking wild horses. Jack begged John to let him go. Denio was an empty 130 miles northwest of Winnemucca. The Denio Ranch grew, cut and baled hay and scattered the hay to feed the cows in winter. There were no wild horses.

Jack was welcomed to the ranch with two hay hooks and a hearty "Get to work." Jack baled, stacked, loaded and unloaded hay for 16 hours a day, 7 days a week in punishing heat. Four thousand acres of hay were cut, baled and stacked in two months.

Plagued with nightmares, Jack would cry out in the night and awaken the rest of the crew in the six-cot bunkhouse. The crew made him sleep in the barn. He couldn't blame the guys and slept in the barn the rest of the summer.

By season's end, Jack understood hard, physical work. He'd never been so exhausted. In a 2014 interview, he recalled that "They just put me out in that desert to work. By the end of that summer I knew I didn't want to do manual labor anymore."

But Jack eventually came to believe that his father's tough work ethic and strict parenting "made me stronger. He leaned on me pretty hard," Jack said. "He was big and mean and one time I lied to him. So, he took a piece of baling wire and he really went at me. If I ever catch you lying again, you'll really get it, he said. I never forgot it. Tough lesson in life, but I never forgot."

Visitors regularly toured the Roddy ranch. John's enthusiasm for the American West enchanted them and his fascination with cowboys was infectious. Visitors presented a golden opportunity for practical jokes.

One weekend, a large-framed Scotswoman in her 60s caught Jack's attention. Her accent drew him. She told Jack she rode English-style but was eager to try a Western saddle. John, fearing accidents, wanted none of the guests riding. He'd given Jack strict orders to let no one ride.

But the Scotswoman was an irresistible target. He set off to the barn to saddle the ficklest horse they had. The woman inspected the horse and mounted.

She wore a long, layered, thick black dress, round wire framed glasses and a large hearing aid. She mounted with little trepidation and settled into the unfamiliar saddle.

Putting her feet securely into the stirrups while commenting how different it felt from an English saddle.

Squared away, she yelled "Haaahh!" The horse bolted. Her black long dress billowed behind as they galloped across the pasture. She lost the reins, grabbed the horse's neck and held on hard as the animal ran wild.

John and the visitors saw the woman barrel down the pasture atop the dubious horse. John was furious.

Jack watched the horse throw the woman into a fig tree. He ran to help her dismount the tree and saw that her dress rested above her waist, her pantaloons around her ankles. Her hearing aid dangled from one ear and her glasses sat cockeyed. She looked at Jack and said, "Well, I'm sure you've seen everything now!" Jack doubled over in laughter and nodded and helped her to her feet. She was unhurt.

When the visitors left, Jack got a whipping. But he took it in stride. It had little effect discouraging his practical jokes or his independence.

"My dad used to beat up on me, so I would run away from home and go live with Lois and Phil Stadtler," Jack remembered. The Stadtler's, who knew how hard John was on Jack, took him in several times.

Phil Stadtler had created a profitable business importing Mexican cattle. While Phil was out in the field making deals, Lois focused on keeping the books and raising the kids. Jack learned the cattle business from Stadtler.

Wrestling the World

Phil put Jack to work, whether it was yard work or sitting on the back of bulls.

"When I was 14 years old, Stadtler had a pair of boots he'd had made in Mexico, suede and with big stovepipe tops. They had mule ears with "Philippe" on them. I really wanted those boots and was surprised when Stadtler gave them to me.

I went back to school to show them off. I was six-foot-five inches tall and weighed only about 130 pounds and I had my pants stuffed down in the tops of those boots. I know I must have looked like a whooping crane stuck in the mud, but I was proud of the boots," Jack said.

He always had a home at the Stadtlers.

Jack's childhood hero was roper Dale Smith from Arizona. Jack watched him compete at the Cow Palace Grand National's year after year. Smith owned the Driftwood line of horses. His Driftwood horse Poker Chip was a legendary calf-roping mount who won multiple championships.

Smith's clean-cut, well-mannered style impressed Jack. Smith would win the world championships for team roping in 1956 and '57. Dale was the first to qualify in four disciplines at the Finals; steer roping, tie-down roping and both a header and heeler in team roping. He would become president of the Rodeo Cowboys Association from 1962-'68 and again in 1971-'72.

"Dale was the epitome of a cowboy," Jack remembered. He would ride around the arena at the Cow Palace in ironed jeans and a crisp starched white button-down shirt. The crowds loved the handsome roper and cheered as he rode by. Smith spearheaded a new generation of cowboys who were educated, dressed well and who turned rodeo into a multi-million-dollar sport.

Inspired by Smith, Jack began to wear pressed jeans and starched shirts. In Jack's words, "They always remember a king. They never remember a bum."

Jack had met Smith in 1953. Jack and a friend had been driving a beat-up old Chevrolet down Highway 395, 199 miles from the Bishop Rodeo to Lancaster's Labor Day Rodeo. Stopping for gas in the middle of nowhere they bought a cold soda and took a break in the hot summer sun. As they chatted about horses and rodeo, a bright white Cadillac with a matching trailer pulled in. Out walked Dale Smith, sporting a white shirt, jeans with creases and a big silver belly hat.

"It was like God walked in," Jack recalled.

Smith spotted the boys. He reached out his hand and introduced himself. Jack stood in awe. Years later, he and Smith would become lifelong friends and business partners.

In the fall of 1954, Jack entered his senior year at James Lick High School in San Jose. He continued to cut class and his grades were failing. Finally, he quit school and joined the Marines, looking for purpose in the Corps.

In 1955, Jack left San Jose for boot camp in San Diego.

Charlie Maggini and wife.

Katie Cooney

1937, from left, Mrs. Burns, Ann Roddy, John Roddy holding baby Jack and Mr. Burns at the Roddy home at 121 Entrada Court, San Francisco.

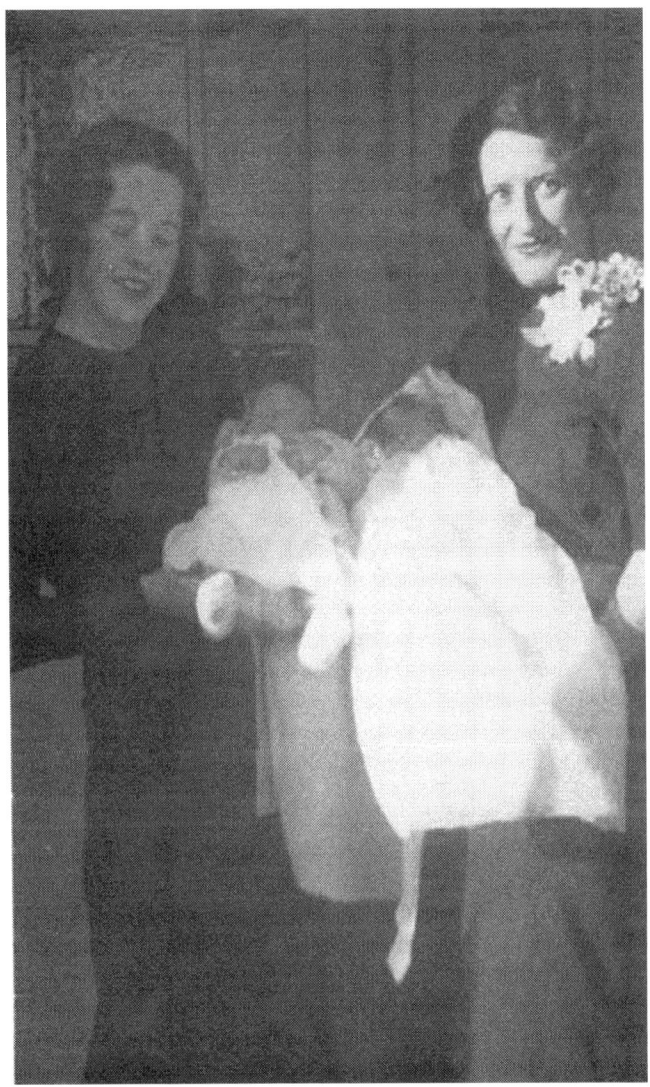

Right, Ann Roddy holding Jack Thomas Roddy born October 3, 1937 in San Francisco, CA.

Katie Cooney

From left, John and Jack on pony Midgy.

Colma Rodeo Grounds.

On right, two-time world rodeo champion Charlie Maggini.

Katie Cooney

Sierra Ranch - San Jose, California.

Roddy family at Sierra Ranch.

John Roddy center holding bridle and rope at Sierra Ranch in San Jose.

Three-year-old Jack on horse Midgy.

Boy Scout Jack, San Francisco.

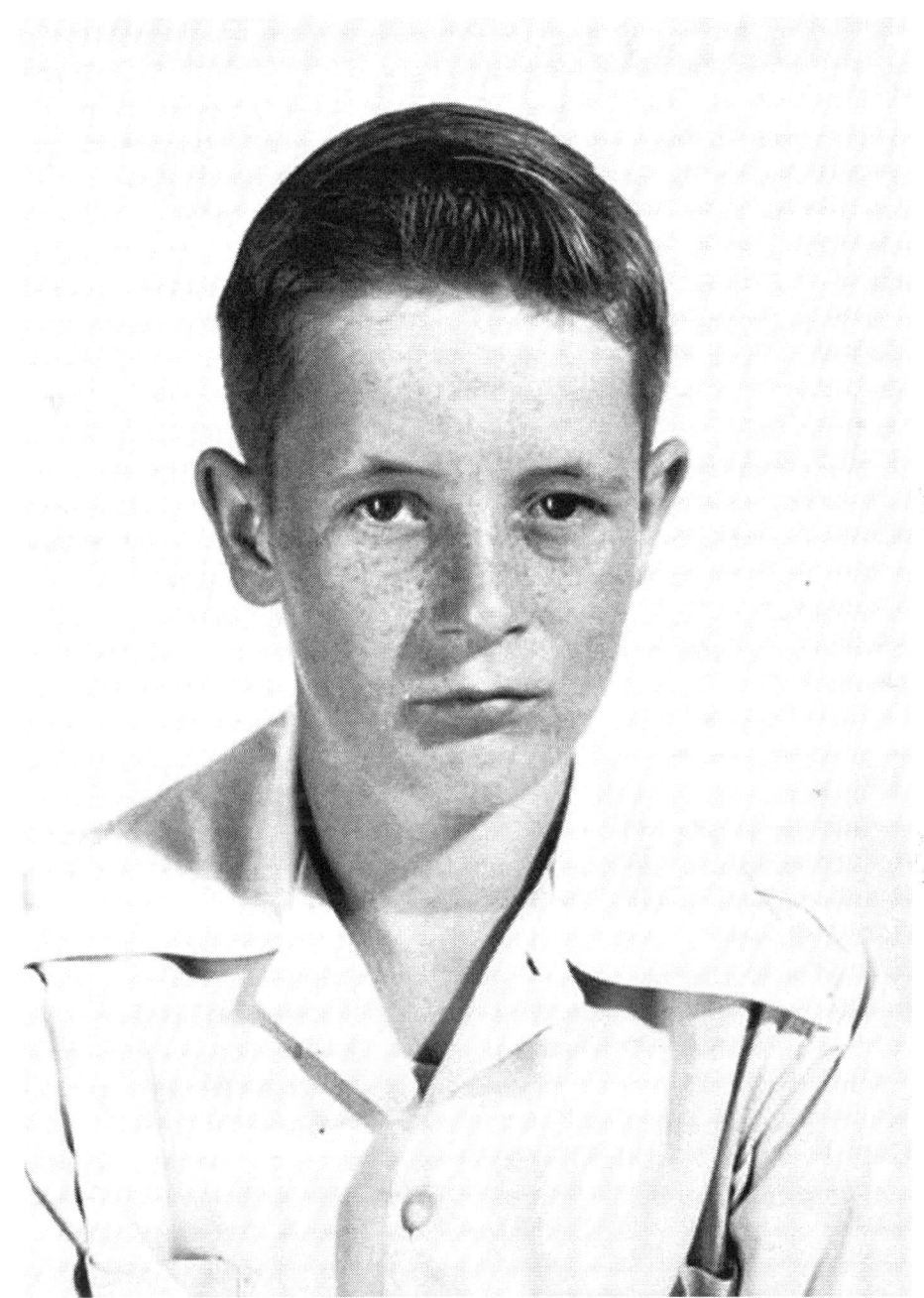

Jack in elementary school.

Jack with horses at Sierra Ranch.

Seated second from left, Jack on horseback, with sisters Nancy and Marion and childhood friends.

Mrs. Michael Roddy on the family farm
in Ballaghaderreen, Ireland, 1947.

Katie Cooney

John Roddy top left on farm in Ballaghaderreen, Ireland in 1947.

Roddy farm in Ballaghaderreen, Ireland in 1947.

Young Jack on Sierra Ranch.

Katie Cooney

Jack, far right, with cousins in Ballaghaderreen, Ireland in 1947.

Champion Cowboy Dale Smith.

Jack, Marian and Nancy Roddy at home on Sierra Ranch.

Standing second to right, Ann Roddy and third from right, John Roddy with friends. Photo Credit: Charles A. Taddo.

Family and friends gather at Sierra Ranch.

Sitting from left, John Roddy and Miriam. Standing Jack and Nancy.

Teenage Jack with horse at Sierra Ranch in San Jose.

From left, Jack, brother Jimmy and John Roddy at Sierra Ranch.

Ann and John Roddy.

Jack in high school.

Teenager Jack Roddy.

Katie Cooney

Gathering at the Roddy's, second from left John, Mrs. Maggini and Charlie Maggini.

Chapter 4

'I'd rather live one day as a lion than a lifetime as a mouse.'

America underwent seismic changes in 1954. The U.S. Supreme Court ruled in Brown v. Board of Education that segregated schools were unconstitutional; baseball legend Joe DiMaggio married Hollywood bombshell Marilyn Monroe; the second Red Scare, led by U.S. Senator Joseph McCarthy, raged on; and Elvis Presley released his first single, "That's All Right," on Sun Records in Memphis.

The fear of communism's reach clenched the nation. President Dwight D. Eisenhower gave his famous speech warning against the spread of communism and the "domino principle." Vice President Richard Nixon echoed that warning, announcing the U.S. would put soldiers in Indochina regardless of Allied support.

For God, Corps and Country, Jack joined the Marine Corps at 17 years old. He prepared to help stop communism in Indochina. The Corps seemed a perfect place for him, a band of brothers sharing a common vision: Protecting American ideals; a group that thrived and depended on the physical intensity of training; a setting in which he could channel his natural athleticism.

Jack reported for boot camp at the recruiting depot in San Diego. He got his first taste of formal training in a group setting and thrived. He found pride and belonging in the Corps and he easily found popularity with his fellow recruits.

By fall 1955, his company transferred to Camp Pendleton. But the asthma that almost took his life as a young boy started acting up again during boot camp. The cold, damp coastal air and physical exertion brought on several attacks that choked the air from his lungs. No strength or determination could banish the crippling condition. He fought, but it persisted. He finally had to face the harsh reality: He couldn't be a Marine.

After three months, the Marines gave Jack an honorable medical discharge. He was unable to serve and regretted it.

He returned to Sierra Ranch in San Jose and John offered him a janitor job at the bars. He took the job, knowing it would be tough to work for his dad. And it wasn't long before the two were at each other's throats. They argued constantly. The Roddy household steamed with conflict. John couldn't stop riding Jack and Jack couldn't tolerate constant harassment and belittling. After six months, he decided to leave Sierra Ranch to strike out on his own.

Jack called a friend who was breaking horses just south of the Oregon border in Etna. The Siskiyou County town had been called Rough and Ready until in 1874, when its 649 residents changed the name to Etna after the local flour mill. A horse-breaking job looked good and so did the 370 miles it would put between him and his father. He packed his bareback rigging and hopped a bus north to Yreka, en route to Etna.

In Yreka, Jack found that the only way to get to Etna was by mail stage. At age 18, he climbed into the battered mail stage and set off. The vehicle rolled slowly through the Siskiyou snow.

The stage arrived in the barren, sparse town of Etna. A few scattered buildings lined the single road. Hardly a person could be seen. Jack thanked the driver and exited into the snow. It was the middle of winter and he was hungry and chilled. He hoisted his gear to his shoulder and walked to the Lincoln Hotel, where he was to meet the friend for work.

The friend didn't show. Jack rented a tiny room in the hotel and got some rest.

The next day he found an ad in the local newspaper for work. Carl McConnell owned Crystal Creek Cattle Company and needed help around the small ranch.

Jack walked two miles to the ranch to ask for a job. Carl gave him one. For the next several months, Jack fed cattle and sheep, fixed fences, irrigated and did anything else McConnell needed. Hard work, but far from John and his bars.

Jack continued rodeoing in his spare time.

When the snow began to melt and spring began to show, Jack's bad feelings about his dad began to thaw as well. The winter had cooled their tempers. Jack decided to return to San Jose, where John told him he could have his janitor job back. Jack had reservations, but he took the job and once again, they were living under the same roof and working together at the bars. And once again, they were at one another. Finally, father and son again hit the breaking point and Jack went looking for another job.

John's friend Jack Errington owned a slaughterhouse on Old Bayshore Highway in San Jose, Salinas Dressed Beef. Errington welcomed Jack as a new employee. Jack rose each morning at one o'clock, struggled out of bed and left the rest of the family sleeping as he headed downtown in the dark.

Each day, he'd find 200 steer carcasses hanging from hooks, covered with plastic in the chill box. One by one in the icy air, he'd slip the rigid plastic shrouds off, stamp the carcass with the appropriate government stamps and replace the shroud. The work was repetitive; like hooking hay day after day under the oppressive summer sun in Denio.

By noon, Jack would have finished the stamping. After lunch, he'd haul each heavy, frozen carcass from the chill box to the delivery truck. Once it was filled, he'd climb behind the wheel and set out to make the afternoon deliveries to local markets and butchers. Back-breaking, boring work.

Jack saved his earnings. He saved enough to travel and pay entry fees for the 1955 Denver Professional Rodeo. He asked Errington for a break from the slaughterhouse to start preparing, mentally and physically.

"I entered the bronc riding in Denver," Jack recalled in a 2015 interview at the oak dining room table at Roddy Ranch. "I was just a kid, way over my head back then, but I wanted to be a cowboy—I was gonna rodeo. I was ill-prepared then. I wasn't a good cowboy."

Jack loaded his robin's-egg blue, 1955 Chevy Bel Air with his gear and took off for Denver. John and Ann still disapproved, but they couldn't stop him now that he was legally an adult.

Jack picked up cowboy friend Paul Ernst on the way out of town; they arranged their saddles and rigging and began the long drive.

As the Bel Air carried the cowboys down the open highway, they ran into a couple of other cowboys from the Bay Area also making their way to the rodeo. Jack and Ernst decided to give them a lift to Denver and on to Fort Worth, splitting gas and expenses. It seemed like a good deal.

When the four cowboys got hungry, they found a cheap place to eat outside of Reno.

When it came time to pay the bill, Jack and Ernst pulled out their wallets. The other two made excuses and promised to pay Jack back if he'd cover them. Jack didn't think much of it and paid the bill but came to realize the two cowboys were broke.

That didn't set well. He had two freeloaders to drive to Denver and the money he'd worked so hard all summer to save was running thin. The two swore they'd get money in Denver and go on with Jack and Ernst to the Fort Worth rodeo.

In Denver, the freeloaders asked Jack to drop them outside the most expensive hotel in town. Jack obliged, happy to get rid of them for a few days. Jack and Ernst headed for the fairgrounds. They bunked in the stables, with barely enough money left to eat.

Each of the four competed. The two from the Bay Area rode saddle-broncs and bulls. Jack competed in steer wrestling and Ernst in saddle-bronc riding. None placed or won money.

Fort Worth was next. Jack and Ernst were packed. They took the other two to the fancy hotel, where Jack dropped them in front and told them he'd wait. In a few moments, he saw saddles and luggage sail out a hotel window. The cowboys were skipping out. They ran through the door, grabbed up their gear, hightailed it to the car and told Jack to hit it.

Jack was furious. He couldn't stand a thief. Jack drove and the bums slept. They'd won no prize money at the rodeo, but assured Jack they'd win in Fort Worth and repay him.

In Fort Worth, the men rented a cheap room from an invalid woman off the Jacksboro Highway, a simple room out of the freezing cold. She was reluctant to rent to them.

Jack was straight with her: "Ma'am, I don't have any money, but I promise you, I won't leave here without paying my bill. What I will do is leave you my bronc saddle as collateral. When I get the money, I'll pay you." A cowboy leaving his saddle as collateral was a high-stakes matter. A good saddle was valuable and vital. She relented and the boys settled in.

Over the next few days, Jack prepared to compete. If he won, he'd continue the circuit.

He entered the saddle-bronc competition and drew a horse named Kick-a-Poo. Out of the chute, Kick-a-Poo bucked Jack off backward. His head hit the wall and knocked him cold. A medical crew carried him out on a stretcher, always a terrible sight at a rodeo.

Jack lay unconscious in bed for two days. Ernst watched over him, worried he might die. When Jack awoke, he didn't know where he was. A few days later, he realized he was flat broke and in over his head.

He called John and asked for money to get home. John said no. He told Jack to figure it out and hung up.

Jack called a friend, Bud Tarp, who owned a ranch in San Jose and explained the situation. He offered to sell Tarp his Remington 30.06 deer rifle for $50. Tarp wired the $50.

Jack invited Ernst to go out and eat. They found a Mexican restaurant where two dollars fed two men. They hadn't eaten in two days. They ordered a second meal.

Jack said he left looking like "a pregnant canary."

When Jack and Ernst returned to the house the bums confronted them, shouting that they needed to eat too.

"You got money! You ate!" they shouted.

"I sure did," Jack calmly replied.

"What about us?" they cried.

"Listen. You guys jumped out of a hotel room in Denver and I didn't like that, number one. Number two, I've been feeding you the whole time and I can't go any further because I'm broke. I'm going home."

"I'll go with you," one said.

"You're not going with me!" Jack told him.

Undeterred, one of the bums insisted he was coming along. Jack clocked him.

"You're not going with me!"

The next day, Jack paid the landlady what he owed her, and he and Ernst hit the road. They made it to San Jose with barely a nickel left between them.

As he drove home, he knew he didn't want to work in the bars. The slaughterhouse job clearly was a dead end. He realized he needed an education.

He applied to Cal Poly in San Luis Obispo. Without high school transcripts, he submitted the aptitude tests he'd taken in the Marines. He was accepted and made the college rodeo team.

The rodeo team was the carrot that lured him to the Central California campus. He was going to be a college rodeo cowboy.

Chapter 5

"Jack is always there, third-base in my thoughts, my mind."
— Monty Roberts

Nestled in the rolling hills of the Central coast town of San Luis Obispo, California Polytechnic State University, Cal Poly, was established in 1901, when public education was making it possible for working-class people to attend colleges and universities. It began as a trade school where students learned hands-on mechanics, agriculture and "domestic science." The school's motto is "Learn by doing."

Rodeo played a large role at the college. Team members Jim Blake and Carl Miller joined 13 other cowboys to kick-off Cal Poly's long tradition of winning at the first intercollegiate rodeo, April 8, 1939, at the C Bar G Ranch in Southern California's Victorville.

In 1951, Cal Poly hosted its first rodeo. Team members Cotton Rosser and Don Koester competed in front of 4,000 fans. The rodeo program was in full swing when Jack joined in 1957.

Jack arrived in San Luis Obispo in the fall '57 with all his belongings. He hauled four Mexican steers worth $90 each in his horse trailer and boarded them in the college stables. He rented a room in a house with five other college students on Foothill Boulevard.

He lived across the street from Pat and Monty Roberts. Roberts had a Western store in San Luis Obispo and trained horses south in Edna. He was the 1956 National Intercollegiate Rodeo Champion bulldogger and fellow Cal Poly rodeo team cowboy.

Katie Cooney

Jack and Roberts had competed in the 1946 Salinas Rodeo horse show.

They practiced together at the Cal Poly arena. Roberts hazed for Jack during steer wrestling practice. Their lives would intertwine in the small family of rodeo over the coming decades. They'd see one another at the Nationals, rodeos, vacation together and enjoy a shared history at Cal Poly.

Jack settled into college life in 1957. By day he studied animal husbandry and agriculture. Nights and weekends, he practiced with the rodeo team preparing for the upcoming collegiate competitions in September.

Later, Roberts would build an international reputation as "The Horse Whisperer" with the best-selling book, The Man Who Listens to Horses. He is an award-winning trainer, a Hollywood stunt double and created the Join-Up equine training technique. He works and lives at Flag Is Up Farms in Solvang, south of San Luis Obispo.

"Jack is always there, third-base in my thoughts, my mind," Roberts said in a 2015 interview. "He's a balance point for me, something I can reach to. That ground-level kind of friendship we have is just off the charts."

He was the only new member to join the team that year. Coach Roy Harris led the team: Bill Nielson, Larry Fanning, Monty Roberts, Greg Ward, Riley Freeman and Jack Roddy.

Practicing one afternoon, Jack watched Roberts wrestle steers with little effort. Being new, Jack wanted to show Roberts his bulldogging skills, Jack recalled. He grabbed the steer and it hooked Jack's shirt with its horns; they both crashed over a barrel. Not what Jack had envisioned.

The previous spring, Cal Poly had beat out Arizona State in the National Finals in Klamath Falls, Oregon, for second place in the Pacific Coast Region. Teammate Roberts took the All-Around Cowboy title and won third in team roping; Greg Ward took third in bulldogging; and Larry Fanning took second in bull riding. Jack had joined a solid team of cowboys.

The team welcomed Jack and saw his talent. They wanted to win the 1958 Western

Wrestling the World

Regional national title.

Jack formed friendships with future leaders of agriculture: John Lacey came from a line of California ranchers dating back to 1870; Greg Ward was four-time National Reined Cow Horse Association Snaffle Bit futurity winner and leading breeder of futurity winning horses; Carol Rose was the third woman in history to win the Cow Palace Stock Horse Champion Stakes and breeder of top cow horses. "They were leaders of the horse industry and the livestock industry and I attribute that to Cal Poly," Jack said.

Jack formed a lifelong friendship with teammate John W. Jones Sr. The Jones family owned a dairy farm in nearby Morro Bay. Jack and Jones would hunt the surrounding hills for deer, which kept Jack in a steady supply of meat.

Jack and Jones would rope, ride and train together over the next six decades. Jack mentored Jones's son John Jr., a future world champion in steer wrestling. John Sr. "was a guy that I admired," Jack recalled, "a world champion and my dearest friend."

Team members had to supply their own horses and steers to practice with. The team had little funding and couldn't provide stock.

One afternoon at the arena, Jack saddled one of his two horses to work on roping his Mexican steers. When he signaled his teammate to let the steer out of the chute, the man on the gate forgot to pull up the line. The steer charged out, got caught in the line and broke its neck. There was Jack's steer, lying dead.

Jack didn't have the money to replace the steer and knew calling home was pointless. His father gave him a monthly allowance of $130, enough to pay rent, tuition and buy a bit of food, but never enough to get spoiled or relaxed.

Jack earned extra money doing odd jobs. Throughout college, he lived on duck eggs. A female classmate kept him in a steady supply.

A new steer would cost as much as he spent on food for a month. He could buy a steer and not eat for a month or get entrepreneurial. He took the carcass to a local butcher to be cut and prepared. He had a plan.

If he sold the beef, he could buy a steer and eat that month. He planned a community barbecue at Cuesta Park. Students and townsfolk alike attended the event. It sold out.

Jack and father-figure Phil Stadtler kept in touch after Jack left for college.

Stadtler once invited Jack to a cattle gathering at the O'Conner Ranch, near Pacheco Pass above Bell Station in unincorporated Santa Clara County. There were 200-300 steers to gather in rough country. The crew included Ted Guidotti, Deacon Hobbs, Johnny Lamont, Harry Rose, and Pa Phil Stadtler. It was an honor to be asked to ride with that bunch.

Cowboys gathering cattle find them in the hills and meadows, roust them out of the brushy canyons and gullies and push them to a central holding pasture or corral. There they check their health, administer vaccinations and castrate, brand and earmark the animals.

In his younger years, Jack had wanted to be a roper. He'd rope anything that moved—his boot in the classroom, limbs, bushes, stumps, pets—he just loved to swing a rope. But that day, Stadtler rode up and shouted, "Hey! You rodeo hands, hang those ropes up!" Many ranch bosses don't want their investments roped or roughed up.

"Yes sir, Mr. Stadtler," Jack replied and hung his rope on his saddle.

As they pushed the herd up to the corral, a calf bolted across the creek and took off up the hill. Jack watched and respectfully remained in place until Stadtler shouted, "Let's see what you rodeo hands can do. Go get that calf!"

Jack grabbed his rope, spurred his horse and took off after the calf. Two other cowboys joined the chase.

The calf cut back, turned, got below Jack and hightailed it back across the creek and toward the herd. The cowboys charged down the hill for the calf. The more experienced cowboys slowed and quit the chase—the calf was headed where they wanted it to go. But Jack was eager to show his talent and prowess. He kept charging

Wrestling the World

down the hill, rope in hand.

Jack's horse Smitty hit the creek and they both went under. As they thrashed under the water, Jack's black cowboy hat floated to the surface.

When Jack and Smitty rode out of the river, he saw the crew busting a gut.

"There were just six feet sticking up in the air, Jack's and Smitty's." Stadtler gasped. "Ten feet, if you count the calf."

Back at Cal Poly, Jack, Roberts and two other team members had packed into a 1956 red and white Buick Roadmaster and hit the road to the rodeo in Tempe, Arizona. They passed the hours telling stories, jokes and talking roping, riding and steer wrestling.

Near Phoenix, the heat was suffocating. Hot, bored and restless, Jack and Roberts started trading friendly punches in the backseat. Before long, it was an all-out wrestling match. Bare chested, Jack and Roberts took turns shoving each other out the rear windows horsing around.

Roberts was hanging out the window grimacing when a motorcycle cop passed in the opposite direction. From the cop's perspective, it looked like two guys trying to kill each other. The officer was so distracted he hit the vehicle in front of him and flipped off his motorcycle. The cowboys checked to make sure he was OK, then carried on.

There was a friendly competition amongst the college athletic teams. The baseball team boasted a world-class sprinter, who said he could outrun a horse for 100 yards. Roberts took him up on the challenge. Jack wagered $100 on the horse.

The baseball and rodeo teams met near the arena. Roberts had a horse under him; the sprinter wore running shoes. Athletic officials were invited to call the race.

The gun sounded and Roberts flew over those 100 yards and crossed the finish line. The sprinter barely got up to speed before the race was over. He never had a chance.

Jack happily collected his winnings.

Although the Cal Poly Rodeo Team entered the 1958 National Intercollegiate Rodeo Association, in Colorado Springs, Colorado, with high points and high expectations, McNeese State Team from Lake Charles, Louisiana, beat them out and captured the championship for the second year straight. Jack Burkholder of Texas A&I—today known as Texas A&M in Kingsville, Texas— won the NIRA Championship Men's All-Around. The only Cal Poly team members to place were Merna Muller, who won first place in the goat tying event and Diana Thorson, who took second place in barrel racing.

Disappointed, the team returned to San Luis Obispo. They hadn't won, but Jack felt he was in the right place. He returned to San Jose for the summer, working on the ranch and rodeoing.

At age 21, Jack won five All-Around rodeo titles and was the leading contender for the All-Around Cowboy of the National Intercollegiate Rodeo Association, with 1,600 points. The year before, it had taken 1,265 to become the NIRA champion. Jack had a comfortable lead. His room was swamped with trophies, he'd collected 16 buckles, three hats, two pairs of boots and three saddles.

Rodeo cowboys know the horse under them is a large part of their success. Jack rode horses bred from a rodeo horse famous in the '30s for his speed and intelligence. He was called "Speedy." Rodeo cowboy Asbury Schell owned and rode Speedy in calf and steer roping, team tying and bulldogging.

Catherine and Channing Peake wanted to buy Speedy, but Schell wouldn't sell. Without Speedy, he couldn't make a living. Finally, the Peakes persuaded Schell to let them breed seven mares to the stallion. The next year, World War II rationing limited rodeos across the country and Schell decided to sell Speedy to the Peakes for $1,500.

The Peakes tracked down Speedy's bloodline and registered him with the American Quarter Horse Association. The name Speedy already had been registered, so Speedy was registered as Driftwood.

Wrestling the World

Jack owned and competed on two Driftwood horses—Jabilena P., a hazer, and her son, Chongo, a bulldogging horse. Jack cared for them as if they were his children.

Traveling to Phoenix for a competition, the '56 Roadmaster got a flat tire. The rest of the cowboys took off walking to the closest town for help while Jack stayed with the horses and gear. He let his Driftwoods out to stretch and graze on the sparse vegetation.

Jack started feeling restless and started down the road. Chongo whinnied and trotted up to him. They walked in step, with Jabilena P. soon following.

Jack knew those horses and those horses knew him.

Life at Cal Poly wasn't all rodeo and studies. With Jack, there always were practical jokes and pranks.

One night it was quiet around the house. Roommates Jack and Alton Pryor headed up to the Agriculture department's Pig Unit with some friends to have a little fun. They rounded up a dozen pigs, loaded them into their pickups and drove back to campus.

They pulled into the Administration Building, scanned for passers-by then crawled through an unlocked window.

They coaxed the pigs through the Administration Building's front doors, locked the doors and drove away, hooting and hollering.

The next morning the college newspaper, El Mustang, headlined "Vandals Raid the Pig Unit!" The pigs had ransacked offices and left excrement throughout building.

The boys were never caught or suspected. Roommate Pryor, editor of El Mustang wrote the article.

Jack's nightmares continued in college and now included sleepwalking. One night during a party at the house, teammates Roberts, Ward and others played cards and enjoyed some beers. Anticipating practice, the next day Jack went to bed early while the rest continued playing cards.

In the middle of a game, the young men saw Jack run out of the house in his shorts. Roberts and Ward jumped up and followed him. They saw Jack backing up his Buick in the driveway. He put the car in park when the rear bumper was adjacent to the outside water spigot. Then Jack started to attach the bumper to the spigot.

"What are you doing?" Roberts asked.

"I'm heading to the rodeo!" Jack shouted. "I need help hooking this trailer up to the car!"

Roberts and Ward walked over to "help" Jack. After a few minutes, they steered him back to his bed and tucked him in. Then they had a good laugh.

Ralph Edwards, host of the television show "Truth or Consequences," heard of Jack's rodeo wins and invited him to Hollywood to be a guest on the show.

Onstage in the studio, in front of the cameras and audience, Edwards asked Jack: "How long do you cook hotcakes?" "I don't know," Jack replied. Edwards retorted, "You don't cook them long, you cook 'em round!"

The audience enjoyed the rapport Edwards and Jack established. What were the consequences of Jack's wrong answer? Edwards wanted Jack to solve a mathematical problem, riding atop a bucking horse in the Cal Poly arena.

Television crew and cameras arrived on campus during the school's annual Open House in April, when thousands of alumni, parents and students descend on the school to tour the campus, watch demonstrations and celebrate the school's accomplishments.

The crew set up by the rodeo arena. Jack's name was listed on the slate of events. The day of the stunt, Edwards stood safely above the arena to watch.

Jack readied himself in the chute.

The math problem was written on a blackboard: What's seven plus four, minus two times two? Jack gazed at the problem and the chute opened. He rode for eight seconds. A pickup man helped him off the horse and delivered him to the microphone.

Jack looked into the camera and shouted the answer: "Eighteen!"

The crowd cheered as he accepted his prizes: An Encyclopedia Britannica set and an electric razor. The razor is long gone, but Jack still owns the encyclopedias.

Going into the 1959 NIRA Finals in Klamath Falls, Jack had a strong lead in points from his wins at Fresno State, Arizona State, Cal Poly, Washington State and the universities of Arizona and Idaho.

With a good chance at the championship, Cal Poly set out for Klamath Falls in May. The toughest cowboys to beat would be from McNeese. The Lake Charles, Louisiana men's team had won the NIRA championship in '57 and '58. Cal Poly's Roberts had been the only one from his team to place in the '57 NIRA competition, winning the steer wrestling championship.

Fifty-six cowboys from 16 states descended on Klamath Falls for their shot at the championships.

Jack took first place in steer wrestling. With that win and the points from prior rodeos, he took the Men's All-Around Championship and the Steer Wrestler Championship in 1959 at Pendleton, Oregon. He was the first college rodeo rider west of the Rockies to win the award. Winning also brought a payload of prizes. He left with the title and 21 silver buckles, five saddles, hats, boots and jeans. He was NIRA's All-Around Cowboy.

That year, Jack won eight saddles, 37 buckles, four pairs of boots, four hats and jeans. The NIRA crown would entitle him to a $400 saddle, a gold and silver buckle, and numerous other awards.

June 1959, Jack graduated with honors, earning a degree in animal husbandry. The Roddys were proud—their firstborn son had earned a college education.

Jack went home to San Jose.

Katie Cooney

(L. to R.). Kneeling—J. Roddy, G. Ward, W. Neilson. (L. to R.). Standing—R. Harris-F.A., R. Freeman, L. Fanning, M. Roberts.

1958 Cal Poly Rodeo Team.

1958 Cal Poly Rodeo Club.
Row 1: From left, kneeling, J. Jansen; F. Anderson; R. (Tyke) Harris; Advisor; S. Parker; S. Martin. Row 2: From left, standing, V. Geissler; D. Oakley; B. Sedgwick; B. Fuller; V. Lowe; R. Eddy; Monty Roberts. Row 3: From left, B. Kasper; M. Smith; T. Mazzacano; C. Leavell; Jack Roddy.
On horseback - From left, C. Kaufman, State Rodeo Queen.

1959 Cal Poly Rodeo Team.
Row 1: From left, sitting, Ray Bunnell; Carla Jean Kaufman; Myrna Muller.
Row 2: From left, kneeling, Bill Nielson; Jack Roddy; Riley Freeman; R.C. Nunez.

National Collegiate Rodeo Association 1959.
Jack Roddy - Steer Wrestling Champion and Men's All-Around Champion.
Photo credit: Bus Howdyshell.

Jack Roddy and Rodeo Queen Bonnie Moyer.
Photo credit: Bus Howdyshell.

Jack waterskiing at the California State Fair, 1960. Photo credit: Milne

1959 National Intercollegiate Rodeo Association
Champion Bulldogger buckle.

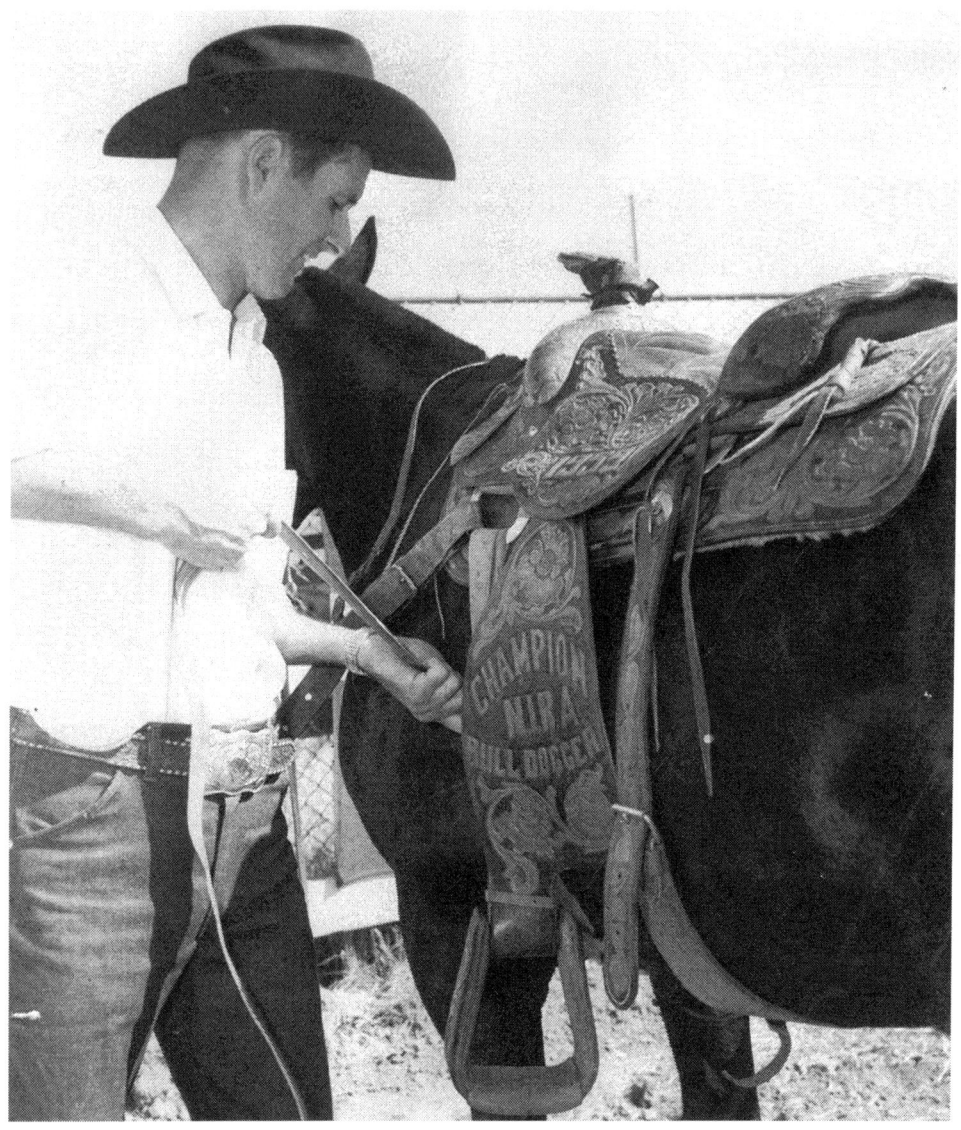
Jack and his NIRA Champion Bulldogger saddle.

Jack Roddy - Cal Poly graduate.

1960, Jack Roddy "dogging" and Jerry Swanson "hazing" in Yuma, Arizona.

Chapter 6

'If you had horns, I'd show you.'

After graduating from Cal Poly, Jack found work cowboying on the King City ranch of rodeo contractor Ray Kohr. At the same time, Walt Disney was filming the documentary The Horse with the Flying Tail on Kohr's Central California land. The movie was based on the life of palomino Nautical, a gifted, stubborn horse who found love, redemption and fame.

Nautical earned the nickname "The Horse with the Flying Tail"—when competing he'd raise his tail after a successful jump. He enjoyed performing.

In 1958 and '59, Nautical racked up major wins in London and Dublin and twice placed 6th in the European Championships, in Aachen and Paris. He led Team USA to a gold medal in the 1960 Pan Am Games in Toronto. Nautical retired at 17 and lived to age 23.

Movie director Larry Lansburgh needed dozens of palomino bucking horses for the Nautical movie, which began filming in 1959 in the rolling, green hills around King City. Through local connections, Jack was asked to show Lansburgh local palominos.

Jack met Lansburgh dressed for work—faded blue jeans, worn Levi's jacket, weathered cowboy boots and dusty hat.

Jack drove them in his '60 Chevy Impala station wagon from one ranch to the next, Lansburgh asked Jack: "You a real cowboy?"

"Yep."

"You rope?"

"Yeah."

"Can you ride?"

"You bet."

"You'd be perfect for the part," said Lansburgh.

Jack would play the cowboy who first broke Nautical.

Slim Pickens, old-time rodeo cowboy, character actor and Western movie star, was the film's technical director. When Lansburgh and Pickens arrived back in King City, Jack was called for his scenes. He showed up on set clean-shaven, sporting a crisp white shirt, pressed jeans and a beautiful, spotless pearl-grey hat. "I looked good," Jack recalled, a bit regretfully.

Lansburgh took a look and asked, "Where's the cowboy I met?"

"Well, that's me," replied Jack.

"You don't look like a cowboy!"

Picken's stepped in and told Jack to stop shaving for a few days and get his work clothes on.

Jack returned looking like a working cowboy. He donned a pair of dirty old chaps and a crumpled hat provided by the costume director.

Pickens explained what the director wanted: "Now, when we're filming, you ride 'er, but whenever I tell you to 'get outta there,' you let 'er buck you off." Jack noticed rocks on the ground at one end of the corral but didn't pay much attention. He got ready to ride Miss Reno, a palomino rodeo bronc.

When the director cried "action," Jack swung aboard, and Miss Reno went to bucking. Jack rode like a pro then heard Pickens holler, "Get outta there!" Jack bailed and sailed. He landed right on top of the rocks and got the air knocked out of him. The director called "cut" and that was a wrap.

He enjoyed seeing his name in the scrolling credits of The Horse with the Flying Tail, which won the 1960 Oscar for Best Documentary.

At the end of each week's work on the Kohr ranch, Jack would hit the road Friday nights to compete in rodeos the next day. Weekends were for rodeoing. He'd won the NIRA All-Around and Steer Wrestling Championships in 1959 and was expected to show strong on the pro circuit in 1960.

At the end of the season, Jack ranked 10th in "All-Around," and failed to place in the top 10 in the other six events. He was disappointed. Undeterred, he adopted a strict practice schedule, setting his sights on the next year. His father's motto became his own: "Never give up."

Jack returned to San Jose that fall. He worked at a San Jose Christmas tree farm. There, he ran into a former high school classmate Anna Bondesen. A striking blonde of Norwegian descent, she was a popular cheerleader at James Lick High School. They struck up a conversation and began dating in the new year. They married later that year in a large wedding in San Jose.

Jack needed steady work to support his new bride and took a job delivering lumber. Then John got him a better paying job driving a beer truck for the Lucky Lager Brewery.

Jack and John had agreed they wouldn't try to work together again. It was too stressful and always ended in an argument. Delivering beer, Jack could work days and practice riding and roping nights and weekends. He was making his own way, just as John had at age 23.

He competed around the state. Friday nights, he'd load the car and trailer and, with Anna in the front seat and a couple of cowboys in the back, they were off. They'd arrive at the rodeo in time to compete Saturday and Sunday. Then back on the road Sunday night to San Jose and at work again Monday morning.

Katie Cooney

In 1960, Harley May of Oakdale was awarded All-Around Champion of California by the Western Fairs Association. Cowboys had to compete in two events. Jack had won the state bulldogging title, placed 3rd in bareback riding and 8th in team roping, and secured 9th in the saddle-bronc competition. He didn't win the title, but he'd finally earned a name for himself on the pro circuit.

Two months later, a miscalculation was discovered in the scoring. It was determined Jack, not May, was the actual winner of the 1960 California State All-Around Champion title.

The next year at the 1961 San Jose's Fireman's Rodeo, the All-Around Champion trophy was presented to Jack.

Between competing in rodeos, practice and work, Jack and his buddies enjoyed blowing off steam and having fun. The Red Barn was a Western nightclub on Monterey Highway in San Jose. The dance floor was packed on weekends and Jack sometimes would sing a song or two with the band.

One night, two beefy men with long, blond hair, wearing white shirts, white ties and navy-blue suits, walked into the bar. The "Neilson Brothers" were a world-champion, pro-wrestling tag team. They'd just competed at the Civic Auditorium in San Jose and were out to enjoy a night on the town.

Jack was minding his own business, he recalled, when wrestler Stan Holek—six-feet-four, 240 pounds—tapped him on the shoulder and asked, "Are you Jack Roddy?"

"Yes, I'm Jack Roddy," he replied. "And whatever it was I did, I apologize."

"They tell me you wrestle animals," Holek said.

"Yeah, I do."

"Well, I wrestle people and I want to learn to wrestle animals."

The conversation drifted from horses, to karate, to women and cinch straps.

Wrestling the World

"Tell me. How do you bulldog one of those steers?" Holek asked.

"If you had horns, I'd show you," Jack replied.

He agreed to teach Holek how to wrestle steers.

Holek was born in Canada and grew up in Michigan. He'd learn to love ranch life from a girlfriend in high school whose family owned a farm. Holek came to love the farm horses. During high school, his muscles grew, and he'd decided to become a professional wrestler. Holek and Art Neilson eventually partnered to become the Neilson Brothers. They won the 1962 American Wrestling Association World Tag Team Championship.

Jack invited Holek up to the Sierra Ranch to teach him to wrestle steers.

"This poor sucker couldn't even ride a horse," Jack recalled. So, he set out to teach him to ride first.

When Holek had a wrestling match, Jack would go watch him compete. Jack enjoyed studying him and his moves in the ring. He saw how to take Holek's skills in the ring and apply them to the arena. Jack noticed Holek had to get hot to go for the win. Getting angry motivated him; Jack figured how to get him angry.

The first lesson Jack taught Holek about bulldogging was how to grip the steer. Ride up on the steer, lean down onto it, grab the left horn with the left hand, then the right hand grabs the right horn. Then, slide off the horse and dig in your heels while twisting the horns to bring the steer down.

After several months, Holek still hesitated to grab the horns. Jack finally yelled, "Listen, I want you to get down on every steer. If you don't, I'm gonna jerk you down on one of them. You remind me of an old woman riding by. If you're afraid, don't come around here!"

"By God, I'm not afraid!" Holek cried.

"Then get yourself down!" Jack yelled back.

Holek focused and got down on the steers.

In 1964, Holek entered the steer wrestling at the Grand National Rodeo at the Cow Palace, with Coach Roddy by his side. One hundred and twenty bulldoggers had entered. Jack rode up to Holek as he waited his turn and found him with a big cigar stuck in his mouth, eyeing the crowd. Jack had a bulldogging bat and whacked Holek across the back with it. "Quit looking at the grandstand. Look at the steer! He's keeping you from feeding your family!"

Holek got hot at the whack on the back and at the implication his family was going hungry. When his steer left the chute, Holek wrestled him down in 6.5 seconds.

A few days later in the 10-day rodeo, Holek relaxed with the other bulldoggers as he waited his turn. Jack was on him again with a whack to the back. Holek looked for a moment as if he might take a crack back at him.

"Take it out on the steer!" Jack shouted. Again, Holek wrestled it down in 6.7 seconds.

On the last day, Holek looked calm and relaxed in the saddle. Jack could see he needed another whack to get him into a "champion" state of mind. But this time, Holek saw Jack coming with the bat and warned, "Don't hit me again!" So, Jack shouted, "Think of the steer!"

Holek took first in bulldogging at the Cow Palace, one of the country's most prestigious rodeos. He would spend 13 years in the rodeo business.

He was one of the first cowboys Jack taught and mentored. Teaching came naturally to him. He understood how to motivate younger cowboys and knew the physical and mental skills the sport required and how to bring them out in young proteges.

At the end of 1961, Jack and Ron Bigon once again were named California's Greatest All-Around Rodeo Cowboys. Jack picked up a state championship bulldogging title and Bigon landed a title in saddle-bronc. Jack won his All-Around Rodeo Cowboy title in RCA-sanctioned rodeos and Bigon won his All-Around in amateur rodeos.

Wrestling the World

Jack returned to delivering beer during the day and rodeoing three nights a week at the family ranch. He anticipated competing in 30 rodeos next season. He also made some extra cash hazing as the second rider in steer wrestling, or loaning out his fine Driftwood horses to cowboys, which could net him up to 25 percent of the cowboy's winnings.

During the year of 1962, he logged 60,000 miles driving the dusty '62 Impala station wagon to and from rodeos and 6,000 miles in the air. Rodeo cowboys began to fly to rodeos which allowed a cowboy to compete in two rodeos the same day. The more rodeos, the more points, giving the cowboy a competitive edge.

Jack continued to compete in every event except bull riding. That was the one event that gave him pause. After getting knocked out and suffering a concussion in Denver and a wreck in 1958, when a bucking horse in Hayward went through the fence with him, dislocating a knee and causing a blood clot in his leg, he still considered himself lucky. He recovered with no lasting damage from both, compared to other rodeo riders.

Over the years, Jack had run into Dale Smith at rodeos. He was the top calf and team roper around. The two didn't compete against one another often, but when they did, they enjoyed it.

In 1962, the RCA board of directors asked Jack to fill an empty seat for the rest of the term. He jumped at the chance to serve with Smith, a childhood hero and now RCA president.

Jack and Smith shared a vision for the RCA: They wanted to make rodeo more respectable. When Jack got involved, the cowboys were "a tough bunch, from tough ranch lives. Some liked to drink and fight as much as they liked to ride and that tarnished the image of the sport and everyone in it."

Jack and Smith remembered well how both their fathers worried about the future of rodeo. John had told Jack, "You can't succeed when the cowboys are walking horses in and out of bars, getting into brawls and fights and beating hotel bills."

Jack recalled the Livermore rodeo; when he'd checked into a hotel, he didn't wear a cowboy hat or bring his gear. They didn't rent rooms to cowboys. Today, when top hands check into hotels, they're welcomed like celebrities. That change began under Smith's presidency.

When Smith was inducted president, the RCA rulebook had just 13 pages. Smith and Jack set out to make expectations clear and spell out accepted behavior. They focused the new rules on appearance, language and conduct. Cowboys could be rough and tough in the arena, but not outside of it. They'd have to worry about being fined, disqualified or ejected if they behaved badly.

Today, Professional Rodeo Cowboys Association rules clearly spell out the bylaws and everything from Conduct Restrictions and Disciplinary Actions to Humane Treatment of Rodeo Animals. Today's rulebook is 290 pages.

The cowboys began to straighten up. They fought less, cussed less and slowly rodeo's image evolved into something more wholesome.

Under Smith's diplomatic leadership, the sport changed tremendously, to what we know today.

Jack hit a hot streak in '62. He won enough money to qualify for the National Finals in Los Angeles. There, he placed 11th in the nation.

Jack and Anna shared another milestone that year: They had a son, Johnny.

By 1963, record crowds were attending rodeos. Salinas counted 14,635 at their four-day rodeo.

Back in San Jose, he competed in the 11th Annual San Jose Firemen's Rodeo and won the "Best All-Around Cowboy" honors before a crowd of 11,000 cheering fans. He bulldogged a steer in seven seconds flat to win the three-day event. Then he won the Wild Milk Race, in which he squeezed a dollop of milk into a cola bottle in 24.5 seconds. His total winnings that day were $758.

Over the next two years, Jack dropped from the standings. He turned his focus on his young family and work.

Wrestling the World

During the early years of Jack's tenure as a board member, a rivalry festered between the Oklahoma and California bulldoggers. Bad feelings and prejudice between the two groups were making the sport look low-class.

The Oklahoma cowboys nicknamed the California cowboys "Prunies," after the migrant farm workers who picked plums in the orchards that covered what's now San Jose and Santa Clara Valley.

And the California cowboys called their Oklahoma rivals "Okies," the scornful slur coined during the Depression for desperate Dust Bowl refugees flooding into the Golden State looking for work.

Tensions always ran high between Prunie and Oakie bulldoggers; both groups were tough, talented and bitterly competitive.

After the rodeo, the groups would gather in the hotel bar and the air would grow brittle, with trouble awaiting. There was no real basis for the antagonism, Jack recalled: "We were all cowboys." Jack understood competitiveness, but the attitudes didn't set well with him.

Willard Combs, was a big, well-known rodeo champion RCA director from Oklahoma. Jack had run against his re-election in 1963 and won soundly. Jack was the newest director at age 26. Combs and the Oklahoma cowboys were not happy that a Prunie, Jack, had beat out an Okie.

That year in 1963, after the RCA board meeting at the Mayflower Hotel in Denver, a group of Okies and Prunies had gathered in the hotel bar. A large fire warmed the room as the cowboys settled into their first round of drinks.

A bunch of Okies were trying to egg Roy Duvall into fighting Jack. Duvall, a three-time world champ, had competed against Jack and they were friends outside the arena.

A bunch of tough Oregon cowboys approached Jack and urged him to get after the "God-damned Okies. We'll whip 'em." Jack saw the brawl brewing.

He'd decided not to drink that night. He was cold sober when he approached the antagonizing Okies, sitting across the room.

"Duvall, you got anything against me?" Jack asked.

"No, I like you."

"I like you too and I don't want to fight. I don't care for fights. Pointing to the other two cowboys, now you two, you're the ones trying to agitate a fight. Tomorrow morning, you get your ass up at the RCA boardroom."

When cowboys challenged Jack to fight, he'd tell them, if you want to fight, come on, but if you challenge me as a director, you can kiss your career goodbye.

The next morning, President Smith heard a full recounting of the goings-on in the hotel bar. He was angry. He lit into the two cowboys and told them that kind of behavior would not be tolerated. When Smith spoke, everyone listened. "If you ever do that again, you're out of here." That was enough to strike fear in any rodeo cowboy.

The Oklahoma cowboys heeded the warning, Jack said. And Prunie-Okie tensions eased.

The Grand National Rodeo took place at the Cow Palace in October, at the end of each rodeo season. The San Francisco indoor arena was the largest in Northern California; Jack's friend Jack Cooke was president of the Cow Palace in the '60s.

The Grand Nationals hosted cowboys and the high-society folks from San Francisco who sponsored the rodeo. The Grand Nationals included a high-end horse show, where socialites from across the country attended, and bought winning horses.

At the Grand Nationals, the cowboys were notorious for getting even for grievances established over the preceding season. After competing, they'd head up to the bar at the Cow Palace, have a few drinks and eventually fists would fly.

Sponsors and wealthy spectators also gathered in the bar to socialize after the rodeo.

So, when beers and bronc-busters started bouncing off the furniture and walls, they'd land on women in mink coats and men in $1,000 suits. The toney crowd was not amused. Sponsors told Cooke he had to stop the fighting.

Cooke told Jack the fighting at the Cow Palace has to stop. Jack went to the board and said, "Gentlemen, the fighting at the Cow Palace has to stop."

And besides the fighting, in 1964 two women had complained about drunken cowboys who'd pinched their butts. The women pointed out the offenders. Jack collared them and told them to show up at the RCA board meeting the next morning. The cowboys sobered up fast.

At the meeting the next day, Jack told the frightened pair that they had pinched his sister the night before. They shrank further.

Board members fined the two cowboys and dismissed them. After they'd left, the directors had a laugh and asked Jack if his "sister" was OK.

With the new set of rules, the sport was starting to look more civilized.

EJ "Doc" Leach and Jack Roddy.

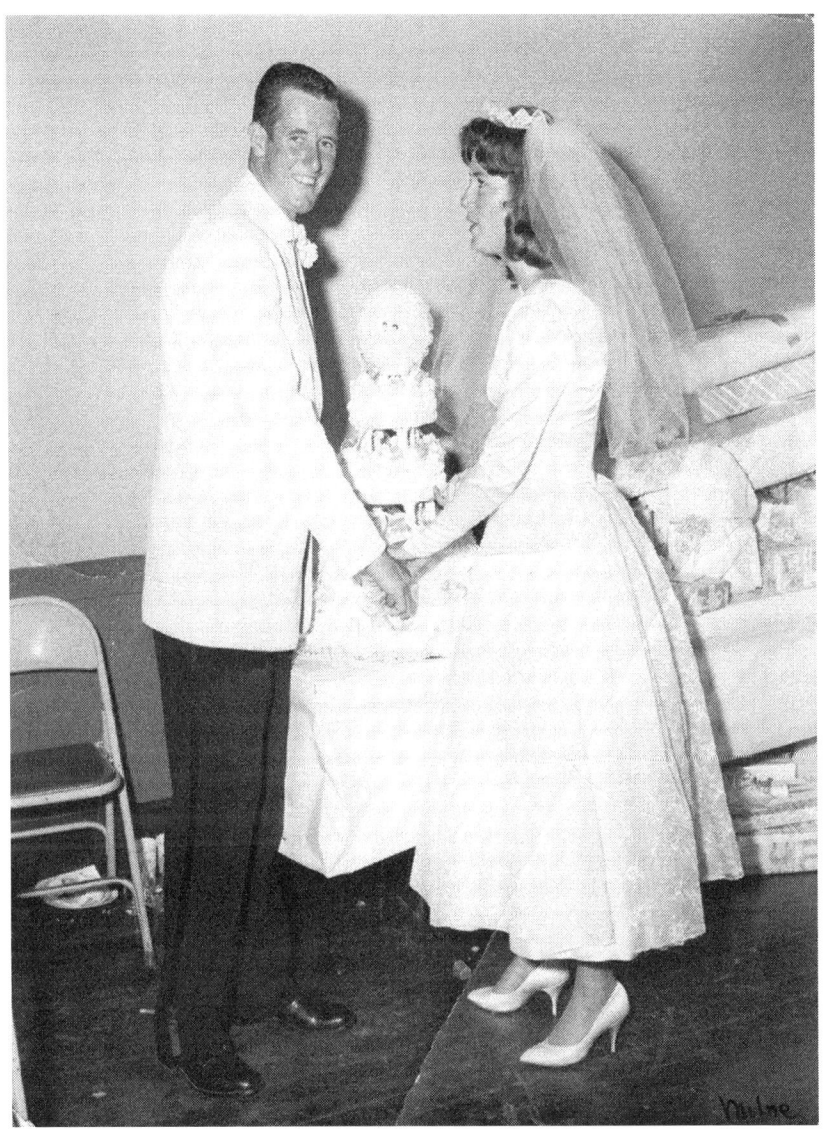

Jack and Anna's wedding in 1960.

Jack competing in Redwood City in 1960. Photo credit: Milne.

Jack and Stan Holek at Sierra Ranch.

From left, John Roddy and Jack steer wrestling on Sierra Ranch.

Jack Roddy holding son, Johnny.

1962 National Finals Rodeo, Jack Roddy steer wrestling.
Photo Credit: Devere Helfrich.

Jack Roddy – All Around Champion Cowboy at the
1963 San Jose Fireman's Rodeo.

From left, sidelined cowboys, Jay Delozier and John Mitchell chat with Jack Roddy at the San Jose Fireman's Rodeo.

From left, Jack Cooke and Jack Roddy on horsebacks at the Cow Palace, San Francisco, CA.

From left, John W. Jones Sr. and Jack Roddy competing at the Cow Palace in 1976. Photo credit: Foxie photo.

From left, Supreme Court Justice William Clark Jr., San Francisco Supervisor Diane Feinstein and Jack Roddy at the Grand National Rodeo.

From left, John Roddy and Jack bulldogging at Sierra Ranch.

1965 San Jose Fireman's Rodeo buckle.

1965 California State Fair Rodeo Champion buckle.

Chapter 7

'I think I'm good enough. I want to go see if I can win the world.'

After rodeoing professionally for 10 years, Jack was wondering how much longer he could balance traveling, working and raising a family. In November 1965, Jack was invited along with 30 other cowboys to participate in the six day second annual Honolulu International Center Rodeo on Oahu—an all-expense paid trip for his entire family.

California cowboys Bob Cook & Harley May from Oakdale entered, as well as, Don Flanigan from Danville and Bud Corwin from Lockeford.

Cook took the All-Around championship and a total purse of $1,489.92. May took home $1,241, Roddy $1,077 and Flanigan $918.

Jack wrestled five steers in 25.1 seconds and won the steer wrestling event and $539. He won $449 in the calf roping event.

His confidence was high, and his goal was clear: "You know, I think I'm good enough," he told Anna. "I want to go see if I can win the world." Jack decided he'd win the World Champion steer wrestler at the 1966 National Finals in Oklahoma City, or hang up his spurs. To win, he'd have to travel weekly and practice daily. The young couple decided he should try for the top.

Over the season, Jack won in Odessa, Texas and in Denver, Fort Worth and San Antonio. Jack bulldogged in Sidney, Iowa, at 4 p.m., then flew to Sydney, Nebraska and competed at 7 p.m. that night. The next morning, he flew to Sydney, Montana and competed at 10 a.m. Three rodeos in three Sydneys in 18 hours.

At Hayward, back in California, Jack won the "All-Around Cowboy" title. He finished first in steer wrestling and wild cow milking and took home $450. At the State Fair Rodeo in Sacramento, he wrestled a steer in 4.2 seconds, not once but twice.

Between competitions, he was bartending at the Boots n' Saddle in San Jose or at the 10th and Mission bar in San Francisco. He had little time for family.

By September, Jack still held the lead. For All-Around World Champion, the rules required the cowboy to win a dollar in two or more events. Bulldogging Jack excelled in, but he had to choose one more event. He chose bucking horses.

"You know, I just needed to win another dollar and I could be in the All-Around. That's as prestigious as anything," Jack remembered. At the San Jose Rodeo he competed in both events.

Each cowboy drew their bucking horse randomly, so no one could gain a competitive advantage in rides. Jack drew friend Cotton Rosser's Pinto horse Cheyenne. "If you got in time with her, she was like riding a rocking horse," Jack recalled. "If you didn't, she was wild."

Jack mounted Cheyenne, the gate was pulled, and they were off. Cheyenne kicked, bucked and jumped and Jack held on tight. He found the timing he'd hoped for. He rode Cheyenne like a rocking horse—with a kick. Jack stayed aboard the full eight seconds, as the crowd cheered.

That ride put Jack into the running for the world. The other cowboys shook his hand and congratulated him. They all knew Jack needed a good ride that day and he'd gotten it.

"You know Jack, that was a hell of a bareback ride," one cowboy told him.

"You know something, you guys, one thing I didn't like about this event is that it's just been too easy for me," Jack wryly observed.

He finished sixth in the All-Around championship in San Jose.

Wrestling the World

When Jack was competing at Bakersfield and planned to fly to Oregon to compete that night, it was a tight schedule, but critical to acquire points for the world standing.

Cotton Rosser, stock contractor and owner of the Flying U Rodeo Company, recruited Jack to judge all of the events, saddle-bronc riding, bareback riding, bull riding, team roping and tie-down roping, with the exception of steer wrestling which he was competing in.

When Rosser's steer wrestling judge suddenly dropped out. Rosser asked Jack to fill in and judge the event. Jack told Rosser he couldn't compete in the event and judge it, too. Rosser was desperate, "Jack, I need you to judge!"

"Cotton, I can't. I'm going for the world. I want to bulldog here and I'm up tonight in Oregon. I've got to catch my flight."

"Boy, I need you," Rosser begged.

"Let me see if I can get you a steer wrestling judge."

Jack didn't want to lose his chance at the world, but he wanted to help his old friend Rosser. He set out to find another judge—and fast.

Jack found an old friend who volunteered to judge.

"I'll watch it," he assured Jack.

He was relieved. He could help Rosser, compete and make the rodeo in Oregon.

As Jack was mentally preparing to compete, the volunteer judge told Jack he was leaving.

"You can't! I'm up! It will only take a half-hour, but I can't watch the line and compete. I'm going for the world."

"I'm not watching."

"I'm begging you. I'll give you my winnings," Jack cried.

"I ain't staying for no bulldogging."

A fight ensued.

Word got around that Jack was in a bind. The cowboys quickly found another judge; they respected Jack and how he treated people and supported his run for the world championship.

Jack bulldogged.

But now, he'd have to deal with the fight's aftermath. It wasn't good. No fighting in the arena was a core RCA rule and he was a Rodeo Cowboys Association director. Les Johnson was at the rodeo and a fellow board member. Johnson asked Jack about the fight.

"Jack, what should I do?" asked Johnson.

"I'll tell you what you do, Johnson. You sign a complaint against me because I got into a fight with a guy in the arena," Jack replied.

Johnson wrote a letter of complaint to the RCA board naming Jack as the aggressor. He wrote that Jack was a judge and had hit a judge, and signed it Les Johnson, RCA board director.

"What do I do now?" Johnson asked Jack.

"Give it to me, Johnson. I'll sign it too," Jack said.

A complaint had to be signed by two directors before it went to the board. Johnson planned to send it to the RCA. "You don't have to," Jack told him. "We've got an RCA board meeting in Vegas next month."

Jack left for the airport with the complaint in his pocket.

Wrestling the World

In Vegas, Jack presented the complaint to the board.

"I want to turn a judge in for hitting another judge," Jack recalled telling the board.

The members burst into laughter.

"I want to make a motion to fine me $100 dollars for hitting a guy in the arena and I ain't hiding behind the RCA," he stated.

At Bakersfield, Jack hit a judge, was a judge, signed a complaint against a judge, turned the complaint into the board, was on the board and voted to fine himself. No one was above the rules.

Jack arrived at the San Francisco Grand Nationals in October with a record-breaking $20,800 in winnings. The former record was $19,700. He'd competed in 77 rodeos, took first 14 times, placed in 48 and accepted a total of 47 checks ranging from $87.20 from Chambers, Nebraska, to his largest win of $2,100 in San Antonio. He broke two ribs in Albuquerque and pulled lose all the muscles in his neck in Salinas. At the Grand Nationals, he focused on the $12,000 purse.

Cowboys competed in 8 events over 10 days to sold-out crowds. One hundred and thirty thousand people attended.

The steer wrestling included 73 cowboys. Jack discovered he was up early. "It's bad when you are a starter. These are fresh steers; they've never been bulldogged. I don't know what they'll do not having seen them before. I have no way of gauging how to ride them," he recalled.

Back in San Jose, Jack bartended, practiced and waited for the National Finals in December.

The RCA had grown to 3,200 members by 1966. More than 600 rodeos were produced in the United States and Canada, with crowds in the tens of thousands and cash purses totaling more than $1 million. The best cowboys in their events were making $30,000 dollars a season. Today, that's an estimated $223,000.

Katie Cooney

The National Finals was the annual eight-day rodeo that determined the champions in Oklahoma City, Oklahoma. Today, it is a ten-day rodeo held in Las Vegas. Rodeo fans and enthusiasts alike descend upon the city wearing their best hats, boots and jeans, filling the Strip, casinos and bars.

Going into the 8th annual Finals, Jack had an All-Around standing of 15th in the nation. After competing at the Grand Nationals, he'd racked up $20,651 in winnings.

His father John traveled to Oklahoma City to watch Jack compete.

"You'll never be as good as your old man," people had told Jack. He aimed to prove them wrong.

Walt Linderman was Jack's hazer and vice versa. Ironically, Jack won many competitions with Walt's horse Scottie, who was considered the best bulldogging horse in the business. Cowboys often leased their horses to fellow cowboys for a percentage of the winnings. Jack paid Linderman 12.5 percent off his winnings on Scottie.

Jack and Linderman were the top two bulldoggers going into the Finals. Each cowboy had eight rounds to steer wrestle. Jack wrestled eight steers with an average of 74.6 seconds. John W. Jones Sr. took second in the average finish with 80.3 seconds. Linderman wrestled seven steers, one got away and ended with an average of 110.1 seconds and placed tenth. Roy Duvall came in fourth wrestling eight steers in 103.9 seconds. Jack placed first in the average and won $1,754 in prize money. In front of thousands of cheering fans, Jack rode Scottie to the World Rodeo Steer Wrestling Championship of 1966 with total earnings of $22,405 - a world record. Dreams come true.

Governor John Love presented the NFR champions their trophies at the National Western Rodeo in Denver, Colorado. Jack accepted his trophy alongside Larry Mahan, All-Around Cowboy; Marty Wood, saddle-bronc riding; Sonny Davis, steer roping; Ronnie Rossen, bull riding; Ken Luman, team roping; Junior Garrison, calf roping; and Paul Mayo, bareback-bronc riding. Each received a trophy saddle worth $1,200.

Wrestling the World

"I remember standing out in that arena and I was on live Wide World of Sports and when I walked down there, I was John Roddy's son," he recalled. "When I got the championship, he was Jack Roddy's father. I did my own thing, my own way."

Jack stood in the limelight and thought, "Today is the first day John Roddy became Jack Roddy's dad." John stood next to Jack as he accepted his championship title. Jack felt worthy, proud, and capable in a way he hadn't before. At 29 years old, he was one of the youngest steer wrestling champions in NFR history.

After the Finals, Jack said, "All my life I wondered what I could do if I performed against the full-time rodeo cowboys. So, I decided to spend one whole year bulldogging. If I wound up in 85th place, then I could say I was the 85th best bulldogger in the world." Not only did he score the title, he was the first Californian to win the steer wrestling championship.

"I'm going back to the bars," Jack said after winning. "I might rodeo spasmodically, on the weekend. My best rodeo years would probably be from now until 37 or 38, but I accomplished what I wanted to do."

Back to bartending and family life.

John wanted Jack to manage and ultimately buy the bars. The offer surprised Jack, but he took it. He had his own ideas of how to run them. John wrote a contract to sell them to Jack over six years. He would teach Jack how to manage them.

Jack worked at the Boots n' Saddle day in, day out for a year. He was the bulldogging-bar owner who tended, cleaned, ordered supplies and kept the books. Jack enjoyed it all, except the daily visits from his dad. John found reasons to criticize Jack's management, but Jack had his way and didn't like being told what to do. It felt to him like his father's accomplishments and reputation towered over him.

Tension mounted between Jack and John. "He just kept picking on me and picking on me," Jack recalled. The daily confrontations turned into arguing and hard feelings.

"The heck with it," Jack recalled. "He could keep the bars. Keep the money. I don't have to be told what to do anymore. I can't operate like this. You can take this bar and stuff it. I'm out of here!" And he quit.

"What are you going to do now?" John barked.

"I'm going to win another world championship!"

"You were lucky the first time. You won't be lucky the second."

"I'll be lucky the second time, too," Jack believed one could be lucky—but only twice.

Out of the bar business, back to the rodeo business, and Jack felt relieved.

He had his eye on the NFR steer wrestling title for 1968. Once again, he had something to prove to his father: He could win the world title, not once, but twice.

1966 Rodeo Cowboys Association Card.

22nd annual RCA Convention at the Brown Palace Hotel in Denver, Colorado. From left, sitting, Dale Smith, RCA president, and Gene Pruett, secretary. Standing from left, Bob Ragsdale, second vice president and Jack Roddy, acting first vice president.

Rodeo Cowboys Association Board of Directors 1968.
From left, standing, Joe Green; Gene Rambo; Winston Bruce; Pat Scudder - NFR General Manager; Jack Roddy; Dean Oliver; Clem McSpadden and Don Flanigan. Seated, Leonard McCravey; President Dale Smith; Dale Linderman; and Jim Bausch. Not pictured Bill Feddersen and Troy Fort.

National Finals Rodeo, Oklahoma City, Oklahoma - Jack Roddy center.
Photo Credit: Devere.

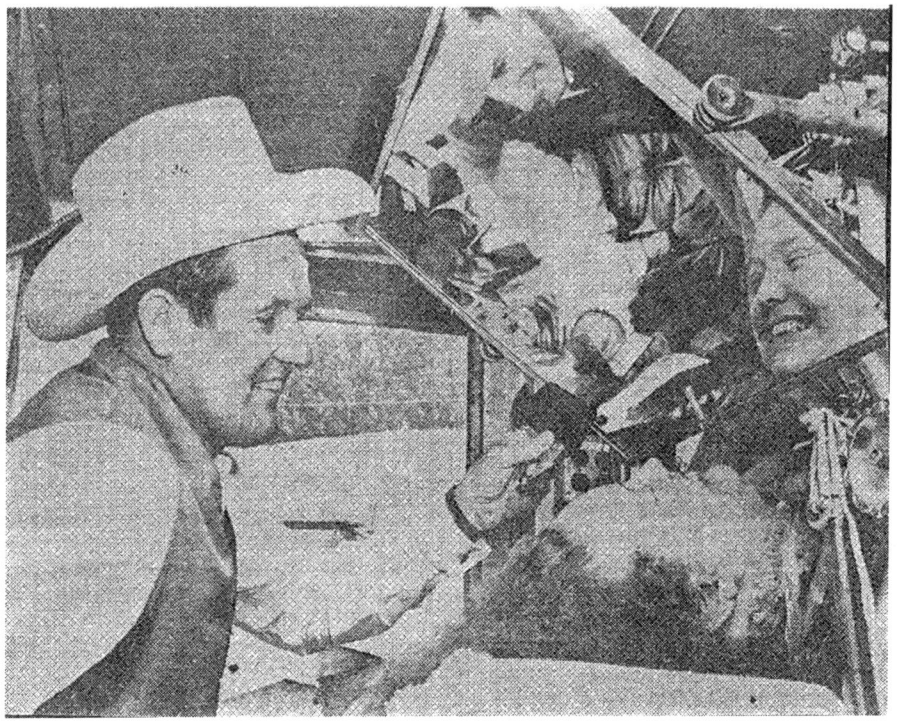

Jack presents Honorary Membership in the Rodeo Cowboys Association to Mrs. Marie Thompson confined to an iron lung who never misses a rodeo.

Jack Roddy accepting the 1966 National Finals Rodeo Steer Wrestling Championship Award in Denver, Colorado. Photo Credit: Devere Helfrich.

From left, Dean Oliver and Jack Roddy. Photo credit: Devere Helfrich.

From left, unknown, Jack Roddy and Sonny Davis. Jack, displaying his 1966 NFR World Championship saddle.

1966 National Finals Rodeo World Champions.
From left, Ken Luman (team roper); Junior Garrison (tie down roping); Jack Roddy (steer wrestling); Ronnie Rawson (bull rider); Larry Mahan (All-Around cowboy); Paul Mayo (bareback riding); and Sonny Davis (steer roping). Photo credit: Devere Helfrich.

1966 National Finals Rodeo Steer Wrestling Championship buckle.

Chapter 8

'Second place meant nothing.'

Back to rodeoing for the World Championship. In 1967, Jack was flying to rodeos, competing across the country and Canada. He spent more time in the air than in the saddle and focused his mental and physical strength on a single goal: Win the world.

In April 1968 at the rodeo in Denver, Hoofs and Horns Magazine reporter Jenny Hurley interviewed Jack and asked him what he was going to do this year. Jack said he wasn't egotistical, but he was going for the world. He'd hoped the good Lord would look after him and he wouldn't get hurt.

In Fort Worth's Will Rogers Coliseum, Jack competed against 116 steer wrestlers for $19,000 in prize money. He downed a steer in 5.2 seconds, won the first go-round and $1,500. The steer wrestling record is 2.2 seconds, set by Oral Zumwalt in 1930. Arenas differ in size, so a losing time in one might win in another.

At the San Antonio rodeo, Jack took his steer down in 3.3 seconds and won $2,000.

"I'm like a guy stepping up to a dice table," Jack said in an article titled "No Ordinary Saddle Bum," preserved in a news clipping that now lacks the newspaper's name. "When I'm in the chute I'm nervous. It's the anticipation. But there's no fear because it's going to happen too quick for me to be scared. You don't compete with the man in this business. You're trying to beat an animal. The guys you're trying to beat are the same ones who help you. We're a close breed and don't cheat each other. These steers were never touched until they got to Fort Worth. Nobody knew their habits until they'd been dogged. But they have numbers and if a guy drew a number you'd dogged, you tell him if the steer turns which away or if he carries head high or low.

We don't cheat because wrong information can kill you," Jack told the writer.

Jack faced off with the best bulldoggers in the country that year: Roy Duvall, Phil Hatcher and Buzzy Kaul. Each was aiming to land the championship.

The Central Wyoming Fair and Rodeo reunited former and reigning champions. Prize money totaled $15,490; 144 cowboys competed, 40 more than the previous year; $1,500 more in prize money awaited. Jack held a wide lead on the '68 title; 39 cowboys competed in steer wrestling, for a $3,650 prize.

Rodeo after rodeo, Jack wrestled steers and won.

He flew between competitions. No more driving all night. Jack placed first in Odessa. With a $1,000 check, he flew to rodeo in Denver. Back in California he placed first at Delano and third in Ventura. In Anaheim, he took the title.

At the Boots n' Saddle, John tracked Jack's wins. The two weren't speaking, but John kept up on Jack's progress.

In July, the Denver Post reported on Frontier Days in Cheyenne. "'Average' money is paid to the six cowboys having the best average time on two animals. The day's best performance in any category was given by Jack Roddy, a wiry San Jose, California steer wrestler, who won fourth place in that event in the first go-round. Wednesday Roddy wrestled his steer to the ground in 10.2 seconds. The sterling performance gave Roddy a two-steer total time of 21.9 seconds and a commanding lead for 'average' money and a finals berth."

In September, Jack competed in Idaho's Lewiston Roundup, in front of a crowd of 6,100. He scored a near-sweep in steer wrestling and added another $1,000 to his winnings. In one ride, he clocked in at 5.6 seconds, a full second better than his competition. In that win, he scored $386 and another $300 for a second-place time of 6.2 seconds in the first go-round.

He won an additional $386.67 and had a combined average of 11.8 seconds, a crucial lead over second placed Donnie Yandell of El Sobrante, California, whose combined average was 15.2 seconds. With Lewiston win, Jack had won more than

Wrestling the World

$22,500 in prize money.

Reporter Pauline Thompson interviewed Jack for the article "The 'Dogger" around 1968 for another unidentified newspaper. Jack planned to fly out that week in a Cessna 206 for the Ak-Sar-Ben Rodeo in Omaha. "Omaha has one of the toughest bulldogging in the country," he told her.

"The cattle are always big and strong, just the way I like them. Since there is a lot of money up, all the top cowboys compete. By this time of year, everyone is fighting to get to the National Finals; the leaders are trying to increase their leads," said Jack.

Public opinion of rodeoing changed when the Rodeo Cowboys Association set new standards for its cowboys. Jim Trinkle, a sports columnist for the Fort Worth Star Telegram, described the changes in his 1968 article, "A Cowboy & Proud of It."

"This is the way a cowboy used to be: He rolled his own smokes from a Bull Durham sack, drank his whisky from the bottle. He cursed, fought, roped, rode, wrestled steers and fixed a windmill. On the rodeo circuit he was a curly wolf and he had to do it all—ride, rope, bulldog, etc.—to make a living. This is the cowboy now: He's a college man and does Marlboro commercials. He takes a splash of soda in his scotch (make it with a twist of lemon, ma'am) and in the rodeo business he's a specialist."

Jack said, "Competition is so keen that you find most guys going for one event. The purses are so good nowadays that specialists are the rule. There's a cowboy here who's one of the best bareback riders in the country, but we wouldn't let him ride on one of the parades because we were afraid, he'd fall off his horse. He's used to holding onto that bareback-bronc rigging and riding a certain way. Most steer wrestlers are big—like myself. Jim Bynum and John Hatley, bronc riders, are little. Duval broke my record last year with $30,300. Larry Mahan won $52,000 as All-Around champion last year and that's the way the money has jumped up."

"Cowboying has changed. We're not a bunch of drinkers, fighters and tobacco chewers. We've got a rule book and we're going to keep the sport clean. This sport is plumb independent. I've got a boy and I'd like for him to be a cowboy. People like cowboys, cowboys don't have a bunch of agents and lawyers like other athletes. They don't have bed checks."

Katie Cooney

By 1968, there were 86 rodeo teams at universities and colleges in the United States, 10 million people attending rodeos across the nation and $3.5 million in prize money. By the late '60s, rodeo had come into its own.

Jack had competed in 90 rodeos by August; including Red Bluff, San Jose, Salinas, Delano, Ventura, Visalia, Omaha, Salt Lake City, Ogden, and Nampa—more than he could remember.

Justin Boot company ran a congratulatory ad "for winning the steer wrestling at Fort Worth and then collecting one of the largest checks ever written in the event, a neat $4,726. College rodeo's top cowboy in 1959, this six-foot five-inch native of San Jose...won the professional steer wrestling crown in 1966 and is pacing for the same title again this year."

Jack earned a record $27,000 in 1968. He had a $10,000 lead on nearest cowboy Roy Duvall, the 1967 champion from Boynton, Oklahoma. By September, his lead was so great he went home to await the October Grand National Rodeo at the Cow Palace.

Seventy-five cowboys competed at the Grand National in steer wrestling, vying for a piece of the $12,000 purse and a spot at December's National Finals Rodeo in Oklahoma City.

In an October 1968 article, "Today's Cowboy: All Business, No Booze," in another unidentified clipping from Jack's scrapbook, he told the writer, "The Grand National has always been my unluckiest rodeo. I've had the fastest throw on a steer and won go-rounds at the Cow Palace, but I've yet to reach the finals. I doubt that any throw taking more than five seconds will win anything. In my event, the difference between winning and losing is measured in tenths of a second. You've got to get the steer off-balance while you're still on-balance."

"The successful rodeo contestant carefully sizes up his steer before competition begins. We draw our steers an hour ahead of our run, so we get some time to study our draw," Roddy said. "I look for the way the steer reacts in the pen, his build, shape of his horns and even his coloring. If he's fidgety, he'll probably bolt from the chute and run like the dickens. A thick or lean neck can determine his real strength and as

Wrestling the World

far as the horns go, we like to see long, flat horns…better for leverage."

"It's the last big-money rodeo on the circuit before the National Finals…there's a lot of tough competition here. Let's hope the luck of the Irish is with me come Friday!"

Jack won $1,895 and ended 1968 with $28,686 in winnings. Roy Duval was second with $17,384.

Jack secured a solid position in the National Finals Rodeo in Oklahoma City.

He read Maxwell Maltz's "Psycho-Cybernetics," and applied Maltz's visualization techniques to steer wrestling. Day and night, he visualized himself bulldogging successfully. He visualized, in slow motion, each step it took to bring down the steer: Readying his horse; focusing on the steer; nodding for the release. Then, engaging his horse; riding up next to the steer; lowering himself at the steer's back; extending his right arm and grabbing the right horn, then grabbing the left; he leans off the horse, digging his left leg into the dirt, then the right leg, and twists the steer down.

Jack says visualization helped him succeed. Today, it's practiced by most professional athletes.

"Jack does not choke under pressure," former Green Bay Packers coach Bill Meyers said in a 2014 interview. "He thrives on it. He thrives on the competition rather than shrinking from it. And most people shrink under that spotlight. Jack never does. He always lives up to it. Jack is the ultimate competitor…He has one thing that no one else has, his work ethic is better than anyone else's."

Excitement and anticipation filled the air in Oklahoma City. The top 15 money winners were competing for $70,000 dollars in prize money. Jack placed sixth in All-Around standings.

Larry Mahan, the 1966 and '67 All-Around champ earned more than $40,000 for the third year in a row, arrived in Oklahoma City aiming for the title again. Bulldoggers John W. Jones Sr. and Walt Linderman also were back, looking for the world title.

"Lions of our time," Jack said, recalling the day's rodeoing and competing with John

W. Jones Sr. and Roy Duvall. The three shared a bond forged in tradition and honor. In the arena, they competed against the steer, not one another.

Jack felt good the night of the competition. He'd earned $28,686 that season, just shy of Duvall's record in 1967. Roddy, Jones Sr. and Duvall all had a clear shot at the title; spectators and cowboys alike speculated on who'd prevail. Jack was ready to give it everything.

A crowd packed the stadium, filling the air with electricity. The competition began. Jack steadied his breath sitting atop his partner, bulldogging horse Scottie. He envisioned wrestling down the 650-pound steer beside him.

He gave a nod and the steer was released. Jack took off. His mind and might focused. He grabbed the steer's horns and they were down. Jack threw nine steers in nine rounds and finished with an average of 16.4 seconds and winning $629.

Duvall wrestled nine steers with an average of 12.01 seconds and won $891. Duvall finished second in the world standings with a World Earning of $17,384. Jones Sr. threw nine for an average of 7.5 seconds and won $2,829. Jones Sr. finished fourth in the world standings with a World Earning of $15,536. Walt Linderman received "no time" on three steers and finished in sixth place.

Despite his slow time at the Finals, Jack had out earned Duvall by more than $10,000 in the final standings with $29,315.

Surrounded by thousands of cheering fans, he accepted his second Steer Wrestling World Championship, this time for 1968. As the crowd roared, he could hear his father's words: "You were lucky once." He put them aside and from the winner's circle, he thanked his fellow cowboys and fans.

That night, a reporter asked him about the interview he'd given Jenny Hurley in Hoofs and Horns magazine earlier that year, about competing again and how he was going to win a second world title. "What I meant (then) was that I was going to give it everything I had in '68. I would go to as many rodeos as possible and, if I got lucky and got in the lead, I would haul hard all year. If I didn't get the breaks and found myself way behind the leader, I wouldn't haul hard for second place. I would go home and take care of other business interests. The title meant a lot to me; second place meant nothing.

Flying cowboy Jack Roddy, Salinas Municipal Airport.

Jack and son, Johnny with dog.

Wrestling the World

Jack Roddy World Champion Bulldogger of 1966, R.C.A. Steer Wrestling Director.
Member of Justin's Advisory Board on Boot Styling.
Illustration by Bruce Howard.

1968 National Finals Rodeo Steer Wrestling Championship buckle.

1968 Champion Steer Wrestler Cow Palace Rodeo buckle.

1968 National Finals Rodeo World Champions
From left, Clyde Vamvoras (bareback riding); Shawn Davis (saddle bronc riding);
George Paul (bull riding); Larry Mahan (All-Around cowboy);
Jack Roddy (steer wrestling); Sonny Davis (steer roping) and Walt Arnold (team roping).
Not pictured: Alan Franklin (tie-down roping.
Photo credit: Devere Helfrich.

Jack Roddy steer wrestling in Long Beach in 1968.
Photo credit: Foxie photo.

Chapter 9

'If you think you're gonna try me, then come on!'

Jack returned to San Jose a two-time world champion in a tan Oldsmobile 98, towing a newly won horse trailer with his name on it. Now, he had to find a job to support his family. Bills were stacking up and he needed work fast.

John now understood that Jack could make a living rodeoing. He also knew Jack might just do that, just to prove he could and to rub his father's nose in it a bit. John didn't want to watch Jack chase rodeos until he was seriously injured, or too broke down to continue. Something had to give in their relationship.

And after managing the bars for 40 years, John was thinking about retiring. He no longer had the energy or drive to keep the bars going and hoped he could take on a less central role while someone younger took on the day-to-day challenges. He had someone in mind.

Again, he approached Jack about buying the two San Francisco bars and the Boots n' Saddle in San Jose. The profit margin on a single bar was slim; Jack would need all three to make a living.

"You've got to come up with $30,000 dollars for a down payment," John told Jack; no favors or nepotism. Jack would pay market value.

Friend Andrew Dezzo loaned Jack $30,000 at 8 percent and Jack agreed to buy the bars over seven years, paying installments plus interest monthly.

Jack and John each hired a lawyer to review the terms. John would receive the payments, at Sierra Ranch. Late payments incurred a late charge; Jack would have to work more than 40 hours a week to make the installments.

Jack made one amendment to the sale terms: John was forbidden to enter any of the bars. "You can't come in," Jack recalled telling his father. "I'll buy all of them, but you stay the hell out!" With the lawyers looking on, they signed the agreement.

Jack drove to Sierra Ranch each month to deliver his payment. He never missed one. When Jack would arrive, John was all business. Seated at the dining room table, John had the payment schedules on each bar laid out across the dining room table. To Jack, the meetings felt like a personal challenge, he said; the tension was barely tolerable. Jack would hand over the check and John would meticulously subtract the payment from the remaining debt. Jack felt like John was waiting for him to fail, he said, but "I was too proud to let him beat me."

Jack now needed to establish himself as the owner. The bartenders knew how things had been done under John. The San Francisco barkeeps nicknamed Jack "Cowboy," or "John Roddy's kid." Neither was a compliment.

Two managers ran two respective bars, one at 6th and Stevenson and the other at 7th and Mission. Union workers, longshoremen and teamsters frequented the saloons. But despite the tough neighborhood, the bars saw little trouble.

The bartenders assumed John had given the bars to Jack and treated him as if he were a spoiled rich kid getting his daddy's businesses. But Jack would take no lip or disrespect from anyone, especially the bartenders. Some of the managers had met Jack and some only knew about him.

Before he took over the bars, he flew to Denver to accept his second world championship buckle and saddle at the Rodeo Cowboys Association awards banquet. After the ceremony, champion Roy Duvall asked him if he was staying on in Denver for the parties. "Nope. I'm going to work. I love rodeo, but it's not going to be my life. I got a few bars and I'm going to go to work." He caught the next flight back to San Francisco.

That afternoon, he arrived in San Francisco and checked into a cheap Tenderloin hotel near one of the bars. Showered, shaved and wearing a sports coat, he set out on his new venture.

The managers had expected him to show up a week or two after the awards ceremony; he showed up the next day. Jack arrived at the 7th and Mission bar that night and took a seat in the back, just out of sight, but within earshot of the bartender.

The closest barkeep was smoking, drinking, wearing no apron and using foul language with the customers and the other bartenders. At Roddy's, bartenders did not smoke, drink or use foul language.

Jack watched for two hours, noting how the barkeeps treated customers. At last call, just before 11 p.m., Jack approached the bar.

"You always smoke behind the bar?" Jack asked the bartender.

"Yeah," the bartender mumbled.

"You always drink too?" Jack asked.

"Yeah!"

"Not anymore!" Jack shouted, smacking the bar with his fist.

"I'm not?" the bartender challenged.

"No, you're not! Give me your keys!"

"Who the hell are you?"

"I'm the guy paying your salary! You're fired!"

Jack walked him to the door and 86'd him. He emptied the cash from the register, turned off the lights, locked up the bar and headed out to inspect the bar at 6th and Stevenson.

Things there were no better. Foul-mouthed bartenders were drinking, smoking and carrying on with the customers. John would have been horrified; he'd lost control.

Unrecognized, Jack watched and waited. Before last call at 2 a.m., Jack shouted at the lead bartender," Give me your keys! You're fired!" He threw him out, took the cash, locked up and went back to the hotel.

At daybreak, Jack headed back to the bar on 6th Street. At 5:30 a.m., he washed down the countertops and cleaned up. He anticipated the morning bartender would arrive and help him get ready for business at 6 a.m.

At six, Jack opened and waited, not at all pleased. At 6:30 a.m., the bartender walked in.

"What are you doing here?" the bartender yelled.

"I'm here to fire you!" Jack replied.

"Who are you?"

"I'm your boss. You're fired. Out!"

Jack canned both managers. Word got out Jack was firing workers and he got rid of 15 in a week. The bars were returning to aprons, clean language and no smoking or drinking on duty.

The jobless bartenders took their beef to a San Francisco union leader. John and the union man had worked out other disagreements about workers' rights, and Jack agreed to meet.

"Jack, you can't keep firing these bartenders. I won't allow it," Jack recalled the man saying.

"You won't?" Jack replied. "Let me tell you something—my dad and I have been union all these years. But I'll go non-union. I will not put up with thieves, drunks or people who won't go by our rules."

Wrestling the World

Jack consulted his dad and got some advice that had worked before. He told Jack to get five one hundred-dollar bills and the next time he saw the union leader, stick those five bills into his shirt pocket and ask him to send some "good" bartenders. When Jack saw him later that week, he tucked the money into his pocket and said, "Send me good men." Good men showed up.

Jack paid his bartenders more than most other owners in the city, plus bonuses. Word got around and Jack had plenty of men to choose from. And, nobody at the bars called Jack "Cowboy" again. But customers didn't hesitate at first to challenge him to fight.

One afternoon in the city, Jack was headed out from the back into the bar. He made out three men waiting in the narrow hallway.

"Where you going, Jack?" one challenged.

"Back to the bar," Jack replied.

"How you going to get there?" another challenged.

"I'll show you," Jack told him.

He grabbed one man's arm, spun him and grabbed his shirtfront with his other hand, then charged the other two. The three piled onto the floor. Jack walked over them and told them, "That's how I'm getting to the bar. If you think you're gonna try me, then come on!"

The crowd had watched, and Jack faced few challenges afterward.

The Zodiac Killer terrorized the Bay Area from the late 60's into the early 70's. He claimed to have killed 37 people and taunted local newspapers with cryptograms and threats of who his next victims would be.

The bartenders were spooked. They didn't want to work nights until he was caught. Jack drove from San Jose to work the night shift at Roddy's on 6th and Stevenson and for the first time hid a loaded .38 snub nose pistol behind the bar. "There was a lot of trouble around that area," he explained.

The Hell's Angels brought their own brand of terror to San Francisco streets. Members congregated at a local coffee shop on 6th Street and raised hell near the bar.

At 11 a.m. one morning, three Hells Angels walked into the 6th Street bar.

"Redeye, bartender!" one shouted.

"Redeye your ass. Out!" Jack shouted with his pistol in reach.

"Can we have one drink?" one asked.

"I'll tell you what I'll do; I'll give you one drink. Sit in the booth, but guys, I can't afford to have you in here."

They looked hard at Jack, then sat.

They all drank a Bloody Mary and returned the glasses.

"We don't blame you for not wanting us in here," they told him and left.

As Jack settled into managing his bars, his relationship with John grew less contentious. Jack proved to himself and to John he could work seven days a week, make the installments on time and turn a profit.

"Dad, the door's always open to you. Here's the key." Jack said allowing John back into the bars.

John frequented the Boots n' Saddle, where he'd spend time with friends and occasionally tend bar.

Jack and John had started down a path of reconciliation. For the first time, they spent time together without arguing and enjoyed it.

Wrestling the World

By 1970, Jack was back competing in local rodeos on the weekends. He'd missed the camaraderie and the challenge.

The Federer Memorial committee, led by chairman William Simas, chose Jack as the first recipient of the Kenneth "Tuffy" Federer Memorial Award in 1971. Federer had been a familiar pro cowboy for 19 years when he died at age 41.

The recipient "must be an active RCA contestant, helpful and exemplify in deed and manner a high degree of sportsmanship," the criteria demanded. "The contestant must have accomplished a great deal for the sport of rodeo and be involved with youth in his community."

Jack was a champion cowboy, an active member of the California Cattlemen's Association and the San Jose Elks Club and mentored up-and-coming young rodeo cowboys.

In 1971, he was elected first vice president of the RCA board of directors.

Later that year, Jack was tapped for a part in the movie "JW Coop," starring Cliff Robertson and Dina Merrill. The movie told the story of a professional cowboy, released from prison after 13 years and re-entering society.

Jack was an advisor to the director, although he did bulldog a steer for one scene. He showed them how to stage rodeo scenes that looked authentic.

"The language was pretty rough, and I complained about it," he said. "Sure, cowboys will cuss a little, but not like they did in the movie before it was cleaned up."

With the star-studded cast, Jack attended the movie's premier in Oklahoma, where the film had been shot. Robertson and Merrill rode in the first limo, Jack and his guests Larry Mahan and Dennis Reiners took the second.

Jack's chauffeur ran a stoplight at 60 mph and broadsided another vehicle. "We spun four times and had to kick out the windows to escape," he said. "It was lucky the road was wet, or we'd have flipped over, probably into the ravine where the other car landed. All four people there wound up in the hospital and two are still in bad shape,"

Jack recounted.

Jack, Mahan and Reiners arrived at the theater a bit shaken, but unharmed.

The film was not a commercial success, but garnered excellent reviews.

Jack and Anna's paths had diverged over the years. As Jack pursued championship dreams, he spent more and more time on the road. And after retiring from professional rodeo, it was the bars that demanded his attention. Again, he was away from home most of the week.

After twelve years of marriage they decided to amicably divorce. Anna bought a home in San Jose and moved out with Johnny. Jack saw Johnny on the weekends, until Johnny would live with him in his teenage years.

Ending the marriage wasn't easy on Jack. In an Irish Catholic family, divorce was a difficult decision to make. However, they both agreed it was for the best and went their separate ways.

This was Jack's first significant relationship that ended in heartbreak, but not the last.

Jack Roddy steer wrestling in San Diego in 1970. Photo credit: Foxie photo.

From left, Justin Boot Stylist Advisory Council; Marty Wood, Freckles Brown, Jack Roddy and Jim Shoulders at the Astrodome in Houston, Texas. Largest indoor rodeo attendance in history.

From left, Justin Boot Stylist Advisory Council;
Freckles Brown, Jim Shoulders, Jack Roddy and Marty Wood.

From left, Ken Curtis (Gunsmoke TV series character, Festus Haggin), Jack Roddy and presenter at the Lucky Lager Golden State Awards. Photo credit: LD Mattocks

Jack Roddy saddling up.

Jack Roddy receiving the Ak-Sar-Ben Award and inducted into the Western Hall of Fame in Omaha, Nebraska, 1970. Photo credit: Syd Cate.

From left kneeling, Johnny and Ken Curtis.
Back row: Anna and Jack.

1977, Jack steer wrestling at the Forum. Photo credit: Foxie Photo.

Chapter 10

'You want to borrow money; you can borrow it from the bank.'
— John Roddy

In the late 1960s, animal-rights activists began campaigning to ban the sport of rodeo nationwide. To start, they chose a small state where they were likely to win a ban, planning then to branch out slowly and methodically, across the nation. The group focused first on Ohio.

At the time, Oklahoma cowboy Clem McSpadden, future Rodeo Cowboys Association president and under who Jack would serve as vice president, got a phone call from Malcolm Baldrige, chairman and CEO of Scovill Inc. and a fellow cowboy. He wanted him to fly to Waterbury, Connecticut, to discuss the proposed Ohio bill. He told McSpadden a plane would be waiting for him at the Oklahoma City airport. When McSpadden arrived, he found an escort and Scovill's Learjet waiting.

McSpadden met Baldrige and shortly after, the bill to ban rodeos in Ohio was shut down. Baldrige had connections in Washington, and he'd called on friends to help oppose the ban.

In 1969, Jack attended a rodeo in Brawley, California. He noticed an older cowboy, wearing a black hat and wrinkled cowboy shirt. Jack was impressed; the cowboy had won a buckle in an earlier event, but he didn't know the man.

A little later, a friend said Baldrige wanted to meet him. They approached a group of punchers and Jack saw the black-hatted cowboy among them. That was Baldrige. The two hit it off and started roping together when Baldrige was in California. They found a fast friendship.

Katie Cooney

Baldrige had been born in Nebraska and was a self-confirmed cowboy by age 7. His father was Nebraska Congressman H. Malcolm Baldrige. His younger sister, Letitia Baldrige, would grow up to be America's etiquette expert, a public relations executive and Jacqueline Kennedy's social secretary. Later, as chief executive officer of Scovill Inc., Baldrige turned a financially troubled brass mill into a highly diversified manufacturer of industrial, housing and consumer goods over the course of a decade. In 1980, he became secretary of commerce under President Ronald Reagan.

In the early days, Jack and Baldrige partnered in team roping. In 1970, they won the steer-roping average in the Denver National Western Stock Show. They set an arena record of 7.0 seconds and were the top money winners.

In 1972, Jack and his friends Bob Cook and Jack Sparrowk decided to start their own rodeo contracting business—Rodeo Stock Contractors (RSC).

Sparrowk, a Cal Poly graduate and intercollegiate cowboy champion, was a first-generation California rancher. He ran a couple hundred Mexican cattle in Clements, California, which he bred for Grade Choice beef. Bob Cook, a winning professional cowboy in the '50s and '60s, had been in the rodeo business 22 years as a bull rider, rodeo hand and general manager of Christensen Brothers of Eugene, Oregon. Friends turned partners.

The bulk of their stock was purchased from Bob Barmby in Perkins, Calif. Barmby bred bulls and bucking horses and wanted to retire, so he sold off his stock. Famed rodeo star Oscar the Bull came from Barmby's stock.

Each partner threw in $25,000 to start. They spent six months searching for stock up and down California. In small towns and by word of mouth, they found the bucking bulls, horses, uniform calves and steers, pickup horses and equipment. They started booking stock for the rodeos at Salinas and the Oakland Coliseum.

RSC partners proved their stock could compete with the best at the 1972 Hartnell Intercollegiate Rodeo in Salinas. It was their first full-scale rodeo and it went off without a hitch. They met the Association Stock Contractor requirement of owning more than 55 head and the ability to produce a complete rodeo.

Wrestling the World

The Salinas Rodeo is one of the top rodeos, not just on the West Coast but in the world. The partners saw stocking that rodeo as a privilege and a challenge. The transition from champion to rodeo businessman came naturally and easily to Jack. "Loved every minute of both," he said.

Salinas added RSC to its stock contract for the big bust out that July. The prestigious list included the Christensen Brothers and Kelsey contractors, a monumental accomplishment for the young company.

The RSC partners proved successful for two years. Late in 1973, Sparrowk and Jack sold their stakes in the business to partner Cook. He ran the outfit for years to come and continued stocking the Salinas Rodeo.

Jack's three bars were doing well, and he'd been able to meet his monthly payments to John. He built a nice home at 828 Sierra Road in San Jose and saved money. With his savings, he bought the Keyes Club when friend Vic Picchetti put it up for sale in July 1971.

The Keyes Club in San Jose was at 10th and Keyes streets and accommodated 40 people. The clientele was Beech-Nut factory workers and San Jose State students. It was a workingman's bar like the rest of the bars.

Jack's bars would become popular and successful because he offered good beer and liquor—nothing fancy, but good—at a good price.

He worked with Picchetti for a couple weeks to learn the operation and the clientele. Jack wasn't interested in changing the bar; people liked the Keyes Club the way it was, a low-key place to have a drink and a few laughs.

Picchetti casually mentioned one day to Jack that he'd need $15,000 cash on hand each Friday afternoon to cash checks for the local Beech-Nut gum factory workers. Picchetti had done it for years and the workers expected it. The bar depended on their business.

Jack didn't have that much cash. He had no idea where to get that kind of loan in two weeks. He figured he could turn to John; he'd been making on-time payments to John for six years and had only one year to go before he owned the bars outright.

Jack approached John. He needed $15,000 in cash and he needed it quick. He figured his dad would see how well Jack was doing: He owned his own home and he'd never missed a payment. He figured his dad would loan him the money this one time for the six months he'd need it. They were getting along after all these years and business was good.

Jack drove to Sierra Ranch and asked for the loan. John took a deep breath and slowly said: "Young man, when I was your age, I had a fourth-grade education from the old country. I came here with $18 in my pocket. You've been to college now."

He paused, took another deep breath and continued. "I'm not a bank. You want to borrow money you can borrow it from the bank." He stopped talking. That was that.

Jack didn't argue. By now, he knew better.

He was incensed his dad turned him down. He really needed help. After all these years, he felt John could have cut him a break.

Jack walked out and got creative. He couldn't qualify for a bank loan; he was stretched too thin and time was running out. He needed the money and he needed it now. He was on the brink of losing it all.

He didn't sit around and stew. He decided the only way to make that kind of money was to jump back in the saddle. So, he scrambled to find the next rodeo on the circuit and signed up.

Just two weeks after John had turned him down, Jack was flying to Wyoming. He'd entered the bulldogging competition at the Cheyenne rodeo.

He had to win.

He hadn't been rodeoing lately. He worried a bit about the competition and his lack of practice, but he did what he'd always done: He focused and envisioned himself bringing down the steers in record time—or at least faster than anyone else.

Wrestling the World

More than 120 cowboys had entered the steer wrestling. Jack was just one of those competing that Saturday night for the purse, buckle and bragging rights. And he didn't need the buckle or the bragging rights. The prize money was $5,000. Just enough to scrape by for a night cashing checks at the Keyes Club. Far from what he needed, but closer than nothing.

Maybe it was determination and grit. Maybe it was desperation. Jack emerged victorious that night in Cheyenne. He saddled up and wrestled down the steers faster than the rest. He collected the $5,000, hot-footed it to the airport and caught the next plane back to San Jose.

Of the hundreds of prizes, saddles and buckles he won in competition, "I prized the buckle I won in Cheyenne that night the most," Jack said. He donated the buckle to the ProRodeo Cowboy Hall of Fame in Colorado Springs, Colorado, where it's on display.

The next Friday, Jack had $5,000 in the register at the Keyes Club, ready for the Beech-Nut checks. When the first five checks came in, he paid out the cash he had on hand, then dashed to the bank with the checks and cashed them. He sped back to the bar with the cash, ready for the next wave of checks.

"I cashed the next set of checks," he said, "and again, sped over to the bank before it closed and cashed those checks, got the cash and went back to the bar. And there it went, week after week, cashing $5,000 worth of checks and then racing to the bank. It was a lot of work, but I made it happen. We didn't lose customers, I just had to work a bit harder and be clever." He saved all his bars—and put a lot of miles on his 1968, light-green and white Lincoln Continental.

Jack learned he had a knack for the bar business. He could tend bar, do the books and keep customers happy and coming back. He took his father's advice and didn't offer IOUs. He kept the bar spotless and threw out anyone causing trouble.

Jack recalled that while he was bartending at the Keyes Club in San Jose in the summer of 1971 a few charros-traditional Mexican horsemen-stopped in.

"We'd like to rent some bulls from you," one said.

"Well, we've got quite a few bulls," Jack said.

"We want some good ones," the charro replied.

"No, you don't want the good ones. You can't ride em."

"We got a guy that's never been bucked off."

"Really? I got a bull that's never been ridden."

"Our rider can ride him."

"I'll tell you what I'll do. I'll bet he can't."

"How much you want to bet?"

"Whatever you want."

"We'll see you tomorrow."

Oscar the Bull couldn't be ridden. The star of all the rodeo bulls in the 1970s, he was world famous for bucking off cowboys in 300 tries. He was small, but at 1,200 pounds, he was one of the fastest and toughest that ever lived. Only eight cowboys ever stayed on Oscar for the requisite eight seconds. The RSC company had some of the best bulls in the United States; at least 11 went to National Finals.

Jack knew no one could ride Oscar. Jack didn't have much cash, but thought John might want in. John said he'd cover the bet.

The charros returned the next day with a brown paper sack bulging with $5,000, the equivalent of $20,000 today. Jack hoped for more.

Jack wanted a stipulation that the rider had to stay on the bull for at least eight seconds, the standard rodeo time. Time starts when the bull's heels hit the ground after he comes out of the chute and ends when the rider gets bucked off. That time between the bull's heels hitting the ground and the fall—or the buzzer—are the longest moments in a bull rider's life. After much discussion, Jack agreed to a five-second ride.

The charros couldn't believe their luck. Alias Arriola could ride Oscar for five seconds, no problem. They'd make a killing, they were certain.

Jack knew Oscar's fierce, unbridled intensity. The charros didn't. Jack had studied Oscar for months. Oscar's signature move was to burst from the chute and spin 180 degrees.

Jack figured Arriola would wear a traditional sombrero. The sombreros weighed 20 pounds and sat dead center on the head. The hat impeded the rider's balance. "It's like tying a weight on your head," Jack said.

Mexican cowboys wore their spurs loose, American cowboys tight. Mexicans rode with two hands, not one as the RCA rules state. Without an arm to swing for balance it was near impossible to stay atop a bull, Jack figured.

The Great American Cowboy, movie producer Keith Merrill filmed rodeos around the country. He was interested in Oscar, the "un-rideable bull." Jack asked him to film Oscar at the San Jose Fireman's rodeo. Merrill sent a camera crew. Oscar made his film debut in The Great American Cowboy.

Friday night, Jack asked a friend to guard Oscar's pen. He was not to take his eyes off Oscar.

Next morning, all was well. The friend got $50 for guarding Oscar, a month's wages for a cowhand.

Saturday, the rodeo opened with bull riding. One after another, 12 bulls shot from the pens. Each rider bucked off before eight seconds. The bulls were hot that night.

The crowd cheered at the start of each ride.

The charros looked dejected. After the twelfth rider was bucked off, one turned to Jack and asked, "Is Oscar like them?"

"Nuh-uh," Jack replied. "He's our good one."

"He can't ride him."

"I know he can't."

Sunday morning, the stadium was packed. Charros, cowboys and locals placed bets on Oscar or Arriola.

Arriola mounted Oscar. His hands clenched the bull rope. Oscar pounded back and forth in the chute, swinging his head. Oscar was ready.

The chute opened and Oscar dove into the arena. He made his signature spin, whipping the charro around like a rag doll.

Jack watched from behind the gates. With another brutal thrust, Oscar spun another 180 degrees. The charro flailed.

Arriola hit the ground after one second. Jack exhaled in relief. "Easiest money I ever made," he said. "Just wished that bet was for a million dollars."

That $5,000 wager on Oscar wasn't Jack's last—he seldom backed down from a bet.

Soon after the rodeo ended, Jack's horse Mercury went missing.

Mercury was Jack's favorite bulldogging horse. Jack often competed on Mercury. They'd won bulldogging at Salinas.

Before work each day, Jack checked on the animals. One morning, Mercury was gone.

Jack searched for hours, no Mercury. The only thing he could figure was he'd been stolen.

For more than a month, Jack searched the pastures, hills and canyons around the ranch.

Wrestling the World

Jack put out a reward: Anyone with information leading to the return of Mercury would get $1,000 and no questions asked. Word spread fast.

Soon after, a woman called and said the horse was in a Charro community just five miles south of the ranch. Jack wondered if this had something to do with the $5,000 bet. He didn't jump to conclusions, he just wanted Mercury back.

That night, Jack drove out to the Charro village with a few friends. The crew included Joe Leonard, who won the American Motorcycle Association Grand National Championship 27 times, the Indianapolis 500 six times then set a track record and won the pole at the 1968 Indy 500 driving a turbine car for Vel's Parnelli Jones Racing; Jim Milton, a steelworker who towered above them all at 6 foot 6; Ray Stevens, a U.S. heavyweight wrestling champion; and Stan the Man Holek, the professional wrestler turned bulldogger. Jack gave Leonard a .38 snub-nose pistol to hold, just in case they ran into bad trouble.

The men pulled up to the address. There was a party going on. The house was packed with people singing, guitars playing. Jack's crew was outnumbered if trouble broke out.

Jack banged on the door. It creaked open. "Which one of you stole my horse?" Jack demanded. The music stopped. Silence ripped through the room.

"We didn't take him," the man said.

The charros said they'd seen the horse in town. They heard a boy had slipped a halter on Mercury and brought him back to the village. The kid was mentally disabled. They gave Jack the address and the crew headed for the house.

When they arrived, Jack spoke to the boy's parents. The woman who'd called about the reward was the boy's mother. Jack could clearly see the boy was disabled.

Jack paid the $1,000 and assured them the matter was closed. He loaded up Mercury and invited the boy to the ranch to visit the horses. Jack understood the boy's love of horses, it's something they shared.

He was "tickled to death" to get Mercury back with no trouble.

But trouble was waiting around the corner at the eastside bar Boots n' Saddle one night.

Jack was bartending on a Tuesday in 1970 when a couple walked in.

Jack had noticed the couple when they entered and got a bad feeling. They beelined it to the bar.

"They were a rough looking couple," Jack remembered. "The man had an edge to him, like he wanted to pick a fight. The woman…also was a bit of a bully. They were both foul-mouthed and looking for trouble."

They ordered drinks. Jack started cleaning up to close.

"Hey. I heard you're some kind of cowboy, real strong guy, huh?" said the man.

"Yeah, I'm a cowboy, but I don't want any trouble," Jack replied.

"You don't want to fight? How about arm wrestling? I hear you're an arm wrestler. How about you and me arm wrestle, cowboy? I can beat you."

"I don't want any trouble in the bar," Jack repeated. "Just let it go."

"Are you afraid? Thought you were some tough guy, huh? Can't even arm wrestle?" the woman chimed.

Afraid? Jack feared little in life, certainly not the likes of these two foul-mouths.

The arm wrestling was over almost before it began. The man's arm had hit the bar with a crack. Jack released his grip and that was the end of that.

"How about finger wrestling?" the woman proposed.

"No," Jack replied.

Wrestling the World

She continued and finally Jack relented.

Finger wrestling just happened to be his specialty. Charlie Maggini had taught him how to finger wrestle and leg wrestle for fun when he was a boy. In college, he and his roommates would goof off and finger wrestle for fun. Recently, Jack was learning to box and had strengthened his hands with hand grip exercises. So, he decided to give it a go.

"Clear the bar!" he shouted.

Jack and the tough guy would finger wrestle on the bar. Regulars stood up and jostled for a better view. Bets were placed.

Each man leaned in and turned their palms up, extended their middle fingers and latched on around the other's finger.

"Go!" yelled a patron.

In a flash Jack broke his opponent's finger and tore out the knuckle.

"You, you broke my hand! I'm going to sue you!" the loser cried as he left the bar.

Jack had a room of witnesses who'd seen the guy challenge him. He wasn't too worried about a lawsuit but thought twice about the trouble that could ensue.

The man saw one of San Jose's top hand surgeons, Dr. Dick Johnson. When the doctor asked him how he'd broken his finger so badly, the man replied: "I was drinking in a bar in East San Jose and challenged a cowboy to a finger wrestle."

Dr. Johnson knew immediately who the cowboy was—Jack Roddy. "I want to get my finger fixed and I'm going to need somebody to testify. I am going to sue that cowboy Roddy guy for breaking my finger."

"Roddy is a friend of mine. I know how you broke your finger," Dr. Johnson said. "I'll fix your finger, but you're going to lose in court." The man shut up. Johnson set his finger and the couple left.

Dr. Johnson called Jack and told him the story. He told Jack he saw no grounds for a lawsuit though he'd never seen a finger so mangled.

Years later, Jack had his own mangled finger. In 1982, Jack was team roping with Dale Smith in Reno. While dallying, his hand became entangled in the rope. He lost the tip of his finger and the rope ripped through his palm. Forty stitches sewed up the palm, but he lost the tip of the finger.

Jack didn't want to pay a doctor to remove the stitches in his palm, so he called his friend Dr. Bert Johnson—"Ropin' Doc" and asked if he'd take them out. Dr. Bert said, "Come on down" to Los Olivos Medical Clinic in Los Gatos, where he practiced obstetrics and gynecology.

Jack walked into the clinic and sat in the waiting room with 20 other patients, all women. They eyed Jack curiously. A cowboy waiting for a gynecologist, their minds wandered.

Former San Jose Mayor Janet Gray Hayes was among those waiting. She recognized Jack and said hello. Happy to see a friendly face, Jack returned her hello as he was called into the exam room. All eyes followed the tall, lanky cowboy. Whispers followed.

Dr. Bert removed the stitches and they chatted about upcoming rodeos and the bar business. Jack promised him lunch at the Sainte Claire Hotel restaurant in downtown San Jose in return for removing the stitches. Jack left.

Hayes was called next.

"What's Jack Roddy doing here?" she asked Dr. Bert.

"Came in for a pap smear," he replied.

From left, RCA board members: Jack Roddy, Dave Stout,
RCA president - Clem McSpadden and RCA secretary treasurer, Winston Bruce.
Photo credit: Mel Schieltz.

Jack Roddy and Malcolm Baldrige circa 1970s.

1975, PRCA creates The Circuit System - A New Concept in Rodeo.
Jack Roddy standing second from left.

Bob Cook, Chet Beken and Jack Roddy.

Jack Roddy steer wrestling in the 1970s. Photo credit: Hal Randall.

Jack Roddy steer wrestling at the Salinas Rodeo in 1978.
Photo credit: Brenda Allen.

New! New! New!

Jack **Roddy**

Jack **Sparrowk**

Bob **Cook**

Rodeo Stock Contractors, Inc.
For 1972 Contracts

RSC, Inc. P.O. Box 93

Clements, California
Phone 209/759-3318

From left, Jack Roddy, Bob Cook and Jack Sparrowk formed Rodeo Stock Contractors, Inc. in 1972.

Bartender Jack Roddy at the Boots n' Saddle in San Jose.

Oscar the Bull. Photo credit: Hydek Photo.

Jack Roddy steer wrestling off Mercury at the Salinas Rodeo.
Photo credit: Brenda Allen.

Charlie Maggini leg wrestling with John Roddy.

Jack Roddy and actor Ken Curtis bartending at the Boots n' Saddle.

Jack Roddy steer wrestling.

Jack Roddy and roping partner, Malcolm Baldrige at the National Western Rodeo.

Man about town, Jack in sheep skin coat.

1977, Bill Gunn and Oscar the Bull in Petaluma, CA.
Photo credit: Eugene Hyder.

Chapter 11

'He got a pilot's license. How, I don't know. I think he bought it at a 7-Eleven.'
— Bobby Adair

Wesley Eade, of Eade Cattle Co. in King City, called Jack one day. "Jack," he asked, "you want to partner with me in a ranch with Phil Stadtler?" "You bet!" Jack answered.

Eade didn't know that Phil was like a dad to Jack. They shared years of history and good times. Jack never forgot how Phil and Lois took him in as a kid.

Roddy, Eade & Stadtler formed a partnership and leased the Gill Ranch land. Directly south of Mount Hamilton in the East San Jose foothills, the ranch encompassed 47,000 acres. The north was in the foothills, and the land stretched down to Bell Station near Casa de Fruta, off Route 152. Most of that land has since been incorporated into Henry Coe State Park. Jack and his partners ran 5,000 cows and calves on the ranch each year, with Jack managing the ranch and its cattle operations.

Jack was running four bars, partnering in the rodeo-stock contracting business, and now ran the Gill Ranch too. He was putting in a lot of miles between his home, the ranch and the bars in San Jose and San Francisco. He wanted to cut his time behind the wheel and suspected there was a simple solution.

The new generation of cowboys were using planes to hop from one rodeo to the next. Jack had saved time flying himself going for his world championships.

He could earn back some time by flying between San Jose and the Gill Ranch. Flying to the Gill took fifteen minutes; the drive took two hours. So he bought a Cessna Skyhawk 172.

Next step: Learn to fly it.

Jack wanted to learn quickly and avoid months of night classes and weekend workshops; he wanted a private instructor.

At Reid-Hillview Airport Flight School in San Jose, he found an instructor who told him it would take six months. Jack shook his head. "I want to do it in a month." The flight instructor snorted, "I don't train cowboys." Jack left the airport.

Undeterred, he went next door to the helicopter airport and introduced himself to a California Highway Patrol helicopter pilot and asked, "Can you teach me to fly in a month?"

"If you can take it," the pilot answered.

"I can take anything," Jack replied confidently.

The pilot looked up at Jack, "I'll teach you."

The chopper pilot handed Jack a pile of flight-instruction books and told him to start studying. Jack memorized 20 pages of instruction each night, whether at the bars in San Jose or San Francisco or up at the Gill Ranch. The drive up and down Highway 101 was wearing him out. He wanted his pilot's wings and fast.

Jack learned by piloting his instructor and the Cessna back and forth to Arizona: Logging flight hours in the air. After a month of study and practice, he passed the written and practical tests. He began commuting from San Jose to the Gill Ranch in his Skyhawk 172.

Jack loved to fly and loved to take people up to the Gill Ranch to show them the majestic landscape. Live and blue oaks grew on the grassy hillsides. Centuries-old valley oaks spread their thick, twisted limbs in wide open pastures and meadows, and the scent of bay trees and dust filled long, shady canyons. Big trees stood tall in the high ridges and stony river and creek beds traced through brushy terrain. The hawks and eagles, wild pig and deer, bobcat and lions had always lived there. It was a cowboy's paradise.

Some of Jack's passengers were less than enthusiastic about his flying.

Jack invited world-class jockey and friend Bobby Adair and a few of his fellow jockeys up to the Gill to check on the cattle and help in the yearly cattle gather. The Gill Ranch had two simple houses. Jack stayed in the two-story house when he was at the ranch and one cowboy lived in a bunkhouse year 'round. Supplies had to be trucked or flown into the ranch; no place nearby sold them.

The jockeys spent four hours navigating the 20-mile drive up to Gill Ranch, much longer than they'd anticipated. "Jesus Christ, what a rough son of a bitch that road is...twenty miles of gravel and rivers," Adair grouched to Jack when they arrived.

The next morning the men rose at 4 a.m. to eat breakfast and get an early start on gathering. As they sat around the kitchen table eating breakfast and drinking coffee, Adair commented that the yipping coyotes had kept him awake all night.

Adair looked around the kitchen for some food to take along, opened the kitchen pantry door and discovered a coiled rattlesnake sleeping there. He slowly shut the door, looked back at the boys and said, "Man, I've seen it all. Twenty miles of gravel road, coyotes don't let you sleep and now a rattlesnake in the kitchen."

Later in the morning down by Robinson Creek, Jack and Adair pushed 500 steers to the next pasture. A mountain lion ran over the hill and darted across in front of their horses. "There's a lion!" Adair shouted. Jack didn't react. He acted as if he saw mountain lions regularly; in fact, he'd seen just two in all his years outdoors. He responded, "Oh, yeah," he responded. "We've got 'em all over here."

Adair shook his head. "Man, I've seen it all, now. Twenty miles of gravel road, coyotes don't let you sleep, rattlesnakes in the kitchen and now the lions are stampeding the cattle."

The next morning the cowboys were again up at 4 a.m. This time they saddled their horses first, then went to the kitchen to eat. Cowboy Joe Maddos finished before the rest of the 12 riders and walked the 400 feet to the corral to feed his horse.

As the men finished up their breakfast, the cowboys heard Maddos screaming. Cowboy Danny Stadtler leaped from the table grabbed his rifle by the door and ran for the corral.

Shots boomed through the predawn air. The rest of the crew dropped their forks and ran for the corral, where they found Maddos sitting atop of a fence post, looking down at a dead 300-pound boar.

Maddos told them he'd been feeding his horse when the boar tore out of the darkness to attack. Maddos bolted for the fence and scrambled up the post as the boar ripped into the fence boards, trying to shake him loose. Stadtler had seen this playing out and took the shot, killing the enraged pig.

A rattled Maddos climbed down. The boar lay dead at his feet.

Adair turned to Jack once again. "Roddy, now I have seen it all. Twenty miles of gravel road, coyotes won't let you sleep, rattlesnakes in the kitchen, lions stampeding the cattle and now the pigs are trying to eat the cowboys."

Nobody there ever forgot the weekend.

Later that year, Jack invited friends along to the Gill Ranch. One was a farrier who was going to reshoe some of the ranch horses. Adair also was invited.

About 7 a.m., the group was standing on the tarmac at Reid-Hillview Airport in San Jose. Thick clouds covered the sky and made taking off problematic. Jack paced the length of the plane, looking up every few minutes for a patch of blue. Other pilots around him decided against flying without visibility and headed for the small airport lounge.

"It'll lift in a minute. It'll lift in a minute," Jack repeated. "It's lifting right now."

The men looked at the sky and saw nothing but milky grey clouds, dense and thick.

Wrestling the World

The group stood on the tarmac for another hour, shooting the breeze and waiting for clear sky. Jack kept pacing and looking up for a patch of blue sky.

Finally, he shouted: "I see a hole up there, there's a hole up there. It'll be clear once we get through that. There's just this layer here."

They loaded the plane with their bags and the shoeing equipment and climbed in.

Once in flight, the small patch of blue Jack had seen just minutes ago had disappeared. They were flying blind in the clouds. A deafening silence filled the cabin.

Jack yelled to his passengers, "Well, I'm no pilot but I'm gonna go up and I'm not gonna look around, I'm just gonna look down. You guys tell me when we get out of it." That shot a bolt of fear through the cabin. As Jack scanned for the ground, each passenger desperately scanned around for a patch of blue. They didn't look down.

Finally, the Cessna broke through the top and they were enjoying blue skies and the glorious warmth of the sun. But it was just a 15-minute flight and they began worrying about the landing.

The landing strip at the Gill was short, barely long enough to taxi or land. Each of those aboard would give a different account of the, but all said they thought it was a crash landing. Once the plane stopped, everyone left the cabin a little shaken and maybe with a renewed faith in a higher power.

Over the next few days, Jack showed the group around the ranch and the farrier went to work shoeing horses. At the end of the third day, the farrier finished and went to settle with Jack.

Jack paid him cash, then said, "Grab your stuff and I'll load you up and run you back over to San Jose in the plane."

The man looked at him and said, "Tell you what I'll do. I'll walk twenty miles and carry these tools out of here before I ever get in that plane with you." He caught a ride back to San Jose with one of the ranch hands. He never returned to the Gill.

Katie Cooney

Jack officially retired from competition at age 34, in 1971. He'd enjoyed a run since 1959, when he'd captured the National Intercollegiate Rodeo Association title at Cal Poly. He'd gone on to secure two world steer wrestling championships, in 1966 and '68.

He retired from competition but continued to participate and lead on the PRCA director's board. He competed for fun with friends but quit chasing championships.

He focused on running the bars and managing the Gill Ranch cattle business. Both kept him busy from can-see to can't.

Jack needed to round up cattle on the Gill and ship them out fast. He enlisted Adair to help. Adair invited Harold Nichols, a tough and experienced older cowboy to come along.

Jack and Adair flew the plane from San Jose to the ranch. They got up early Tuesday and readied for a long day of gathering cattle, but Jack couldn't find the keys for the pasture gates.

Each pasture on the ranch was fenced with a locked gate. This ensured cattle from different ranches grazing on the land wouldn't get mixed up or lost and kept hunters, partiers and sightseers out. Jack had forgotten the keys in San Jose. Eight big cattle trucks were due the next day to haul the cattle away. Everyone was waiting to get started, but without the keys, they were stuck.

Jack told them to saddle the horses and get ready to gather. He and Adair were going to hop over to San Jose and have his attorney bring a second set of keys to the Reid-Hillview Airport. Jack told the cowboys he'd buzz the corrals on the way back and whoever was in the pickup truck could pick them up at the landing strip.

Jack and Adair boarded the plane. Jack pushed the plane down the bumpy dirt runway and took to the sky.

They landed in San Jose and waited for the keys. Few people were around.

The lawyer finally arrived, and they flew out for the Gill Ranch.

Wrestling the World

It was springtime and the wind in the valley was up a bit more than usual that morning.

Jack buzzed the corrals to alert one of those below and Adair's friend Nichols headed for the strip in the truck.

Jack circled the strip as Nichols drove up and got out to watch. Jack descended, but just before he touched down a gust of wind swept under and pushed them right back into the sky.

It took them all by surprise. Jack figured he needed a bit more speed to compensate for the wind. He circled and headed down for the strip once again. And again, the wind caught them and forced them back into the sky.

Nichols stood next to one of the barbed-wire fences that lined the landing strip, watching Jack trying to land. Down the plane came for the third time and, as before, the plane caught a gust and popped straight back skyward. Jack got mad.

"I think you need to give it some gas," Adair said.

Sweat was coming off Jack's forehead as he circled again. He finally shouted, "Buckle up! We're going down no matter what!"

Jack flew the plane down, down, down and slammed it to the runway. It continued straight into the pasture toward the tree line, just missing barbed wire and ditches. It was as near as you could get to a crash landing. A slack-jawed Nichols watched the whole thing.

The men headed back to the corral in the pickup, boarded their horses and joined the gather. By nightfall they'd finished. The cattle were corralled, waiting for the morning trucks.

Wednesday, the cowboys were up early again, out saddling up before sunrise, waiting for the trucks. Thirteen rigs made their way into the deep valley on time and the crew prepared to load 910 steers.

Nichols was an experienced cowhand, a bit older than the rest of the crew, but big and strong as Jack. He was riding a beautiful 5-year-old mare, one of his younger horses he was training to work cattle.

Nichols took the lead, expertly pushing the steers into the trucks. The cattle, full and fat, weighed 700-800 pounds each. As they moved up the chute to the truck, one abruptly turned in the chute and lunged back toward him. Nichols hollered and rode close to turn it, but the steer charged under his horse. The horse threw Nichols who struck his head on an oak tree.

Everything stopped when Nichols hit the dirt. They all ran to help him. He was unmoving and they thought he was dead. No one spoke. The ranch had no phone; they couldn't call for help.

Nichols was out cold for nearly an hour. He lay there and the men just stood by and watched. Jack finally couldn't take it any longer. "Hey guys, pick him up and load him into the back of the pickup, I'm going to fly him to the hospital in San Jose."

Just then, Nichols began to regain consciousness. "Bobby, Bobby," he moaned to Adair. "If I'm going to die, I'll die right here. I'm not getting on that plane."

Nichols regained his senses and caught a ride back with the cattle trucks. He never again got in Jack's plane.

Many cowboys and friends came to the Gill for a short or extended visit, but all left with memorable stories.

Jack had a couple of men working the Gill Ranch year-round. They tended cattle, repaired fences and looked after the land. He'd fly down once a week to check in, stock the kitchen food and beer and work cattle.

In 1972, New Zealander Davey Oakes went to working for him. "Mate," he said to Jack, "I've got a young girl I'm dating. Could she come spend a week at the ranch with me?"

"Well, sure," Jack told him.

Wrestling the World

Oakes met her at the San Jose Airport and drove her to the ranch. They spent the week together and on Jack's weekly visit, Oakes asked him if he'd fly his girlfriend back to San Jose. Jack was happy to help.

Over the week, she'd heard some of Jack's flying adventures, but wasn't sure whether the men were pulling her leg, or she really should be concerned. But she needed to catch her flight back home.

She climbed aboard for her first flight in a light plane and Jack sensed her anxiety.

She started asking questions about flying and safety. Jack calmly told her, "Don't worry, honey. I can fly this plane."

She settled into her seat, reassured but not completely at ease.

About 10 minutes from Reid-Hillview Airport, she seemed relaxed, enjoying the ride until she noticed the gas gauge was on empty. She pointed and asked, "Is that your gas?"

"Yeah," Jack replied.

"You're outta gas!" she shrieked.

The gas gauge was on "E," but Jack knew the Cessna had at least an hour of fuel left. He saw a golden opportunity.

He put a concerned look on his face; "Oh my gosh, we're outta gas!"

"Are we gonna crash?" she cried.

"Honey, don't worry."

He picked up his microphone and pretended to send a distress call.

"Reid-Hillview tower, a mile south of Mount Hamilton at 4,000 feet. Running short of fuel, will attempt to make the airport."

Katie Cooney

She grabbed onto her seat, waiting for the imminent crash.

At the five-mile marker, planes are required to reduce power for landing. Jack reduced the plane's power and acted as if they'd run dry.

"Are we out of gas?"

"Baby, that's it."

"What are we gonna do?"

"Look for a place to land."

She scanned the landscape—nothing but hills. "I don't see anywhere to land," she told him.

"Keep looking!" he urged.

Side to side she frantically scanned, looking for room. "There's houses down there!"

"Find a flat place to land," he repeated. She kept up her desperate search.

Finally, they were near Reid-Hillview, an airport so small she didn't notice it. The plane descended, lower and lower.

"What are we gonna do?" she cried.

Jack turned to her and told her solemnly, "Honey, put your head between your legs."

"Then what?" she asked.

"Kiss your ass goodbye!" Jack said with a wink and a smile.

Jack couldn't stop laughing as he landed routinely. She never stopped swearing as she opened the door, walked across the tarmac and out of his life. He never saw her again.

Wrestling the World

Years later, Jack recalled he'd never heard a woman use such language.

Juggling the bars and managing the Gill Ranch, Jack continued to serve on the Rodeo Cowboys Association board of directors.

Cowboys sought Jack's help when they needed advice. Jack helped a fellow cowboy we'll call "Butch", after he had threatened a judge and got tagged with a $5,000 penalty bond. He couldn't compete until he paid it. Jack told Butch to join him at the RCA directors' meeting and he'd try to persuade the board to lift the bond. Butch threatened the board at the meeting. Unsurprisingly, the bond stayed.

At Oregon's Pendleton Rodeo in 1972, Jack caught up with friends at the hotel bar. Butch was there talking bad about the RCA board. Jack approached him.

"Butch, I heard you cussed the RCA board. You called 'em a bunch of jerks."

"Yeah. I sure did," Butch said.

"Butch, I'm on that board."

"Well, I guess you're one of them."

A fight ensued. Butch grabbed Jack around the neck and rammed his head into the cigarette machine. Blinded by blood, Jack fell to the floor and Butch ran. Cowboys pursued. They brought him back and waited for the cops. Jack went to the hospital for stitches.

At the next board of directors meeting, president Dale Smith started "Jack, we all heard about your fight in Pendleton and we feel a guy like you, who's well-known and respected in our industry, who got into a bar room brawl in Pendleton, is something we…well, we don't care for."

The rest of the directors sat straight-faced, avoiding Jack's gaze.

Smith kept lecturing and Jack grew angry. "Hell," he thought. "I was defending all these guys."

"Whoa, Dale," Clem McSpadden, the board's vice president interrupted Smith. Smith turned to Jack and gave a smile. The board broke into laughter.

Jack was presented a trophy. The plaque read: "To Jack L. Roddy for bravery above and beyond the call of duty. Pendleton Oregon, 1972, The Ranch, RCA Board of Directors." The "L" was a nod to the first heavyweight boxing champion John L. Sullivan. The trophy's cup was full of half and silver dollars, to pay for the stitches.

That trophy is on display at the ProRodeo Hall of Fame in Colorado Springs.

In 1973, Jack met Julie Herrin, a San Jose native and single mother. She and her young son Jerry lived in San Jose. Herrin tended bar at the Boots n' Saddle. Jack taught her how to ride and they discovered her natural talent for rodeo.

They married in 1976. Jack ran the cattle business and Julie trained, practiced and dreamed of being a professional rodeo cowgirl. During her career, she'd win over a $1 million dollars roping and riding.

The Gill Ranch was a place for adventure and antics. If you survived the plane ride, chances were you'd had a memorable time.

One weekend, Jack set out to make his rounds. He saw a cow lying senseless under a tree about 10 miles from the house. She had just given birth to a small, weak calf.

Jack slowly approached and checked the cow. She was dead. The calf didn't have a chance among the coyotes, lions and other predators. Jack zipped her into his leather jacket and mounted up, with the calf calmly nestled into his jacket. He named her Kathy and bottle-fed her until she could graze.

Friend and rodeo clown Jerry Mariluch had a pet coyote named Wiley. Jerry was moving to Oregon and Wiley needed a new home. Mariluch asked Jack to take him and Jack said, "Sure."

Jack flew Wiley up to the Gill, where he had a couple of good cow dogs. One named Whiskey took up with Wiley.

Wrestling the World

After they adopted Wiley, Julie found an abandoned fawn and they decided to raise it, too. They bottle-fed her until she was strong enough to get along.

Jack flew back to his San Jose home with Whiskey the dog, Wiley the coyote, Kathy the calf and Bambi the fawn.

The Reid-Hillview Airport staff watched Jack unload his menagerie. They teased him about "running a zoo."

Wiley the coyote commuted to and from the Gill. He worked cattle and explored the hills. He'd wander farther and farther each time and after three months he went back to the wild.

Bambi followed Jack and Julie like a puppy. She'd swim in the lake with Johnny and Jerry.

One day, Julie and Bambi were out checking cattle. Julie tied her to a trailer.

The cattle spooked her, and she slipped the tie and ran off. A resident spotted her. They called the game warden.

Jack found out the Fish & Game department had Bambi. The state wouldn't put a wild animal back into a domesticated situation and the family mourned her loss.

Years later, Whiskey contracted distemper and was put down. The leppy calf Kathy died at 16.

Jack, Julie and the kids flew to the ranch one Friday. He had to check cattle and wanted to have some fun with the family. He'd promised the San Jose Police chief he'd speak at the San Jose Elks Club at noon Monday.

Monday morning, fog lay heavy on the hills; visibility was zero. But they ate breakfast and packed up. He'd seen fog before and was sure this would lift.

Jack and Julie waited for blue skies as the boys goofed off. Jack always kept his promises and if he drove, he'd miss the meeting. No way to call.

Jack spied what pilots aptly called a "sucker hole." He said to Julie, "Come on, we'll make it."

They boarded the plane, took off down the runway and broke into the blue sky.

Nearing the Reid-Hillview Airport, Jack headed toward another sucker hole. He nosed the plane down through the cloud. "Now, a good pilot would've just taken the plane and spiraled, circled through it," Jack recalled in a 2016 interview. "Instead, I nosed it down."

Panic set in as they hit 180 mph. Jack pulled back the yoke; at 200 mph, the wings would tear off. "If you ever get in trouble, the helicopter pilot had taught him, turn loose of the plane; it wants to fly itself." Jack turned it loose.

At 1,500 feet, they emerged. Mount Hamilton stood a half-mile off. Any closer and they'd have crashed into it. Jack was terrified.

Julie never flew with him again.

Tending bar at the Keyes Club in San Jose, Jack met crowds of people from all walks of life. He befriended one man named Red. Red had just gotten out of prison on a manslaughter charge when he started frequenting the Keyes.

He said he was a former Hell's Angel who'd disassociated himself from the gang on his release from prison. Red said he wanted a fresh start. He'd heard about the Gill Ranch from Jack and others at the bar. It sounded ideal for him to get away and work back into life outside prison.

"Jack, I'd like to go up with you someday to see the ranch," he said one day in late 1972.

"Sure," Jack said.

A few weeks later, loaded up with supplies, they flew to the Gill. After a day at the ranch, Red told Jack, "I'll tell you what I'd love to do. I'd love to stay up here. I don't need any money and I can't ride a horse, but I can fix stuff. I just want to get away

Wrestling the World

from people."

"Red, I'll furnish your food and I'll pay you a little bit," Jack said.

Red stayed a couple months. He appreciated the solitude and open space.

When Jack took his boys Johnny and Jerry up to the Gill, Red took them fishing.

Cowboys would come and go at the Gill with the seasons. A lot of guys didn't want to stay on too long at the isolated ranch. Jack got a call one day in March 1974 from a puncher we'll call "Hitch," and Hitch wanted a job. Jack needed another hand and told him he'd put him to work.

Jack told him, "All I want you to do is just saddle up and ride through the cattle. Next month, we'll start moving and sorting."

He showed up at the Gill Ranch and went to work with Red. All seemed well.

St. Patrick's Day was a celebration at the bars. Jack handed out free corned beef sandwiches all day. People came from San Francisco to San Jose to party. The bars were packed.

Red remembered Jack's stories of St. Patrick's Day at the Boots n' Saddle and the free sandwiches. He asked Jack if it would be OK if he and Hitch came to the bar. That was fine by Jack.

For a St. Paddy's Day prank, Jack called up a gal he'd dated a couple of times who worked in the Sheriff's Office and asked her to streak the Boots n' Saddle at noon. Streaking naked through a public event was popular for show or protest in the '70s. Jack asked her to dye herself green and wear green panties when she ran through the bar.

She was up for it and she left work to go home and soak in a bathtub of green dye. A friend picked her up and took her to the bar at noon.

When Jack opened the Boots n' Saddle at 6 a.m. that day, he turned on the bar's television for the local news. The station reported a murder. Word reached Jack that Hitch had slit Red's throat the night before in Mountain View. The killing threw the entire bar into a state of shock. Red was known and liked by many.

Just before noon, two detectives showed up, wanting to ask Jack some questions about Red and Hitch. Jack was explaining the situation to the cops when one of them shouted, "Look!" The three turned to see a green woman running naked through the bar. The crowd cheered and roared.

Jack turned to one of the detectives, whom he knew, and said, "Detective, don't believe your lying eyes."

Jack later mused that the Boots n' Saddle was the only place around that would have a murder and a girl streaking green the same day.

Jack was never quite sure what happened between the two men. He heard something about self-defense. Jack had no further contact with the case. Hitch went back to Montana and Jack never saw or spoke to him again.

Bobby Adair, professional jockey and horseman.
Photo credit: Bill McNabb Jr.

Rounding up cattle on the Gill Ranch in San Jose, CA.

Chapter 12

'Rancheros Vistadores is a group of brilliant men who work all year to be little boys for a week.'

Early each May since 1929, 700 of the country's most powerful and elite men have descended into the Santa Ynez Valley near Santa Barbara for an invitation-only, exclusive all-male trail ride. For a week, the Rancheros Vistadores, or "Visiting Ranchers," ride through the Santa Ynez Mountains, share stories, perform skits, horse around, drink, race their horses, rope and shoot, and brand calves and anything else that might cross their paths.

Prospective members are invited three times, then placed on a waiting list—a virtual who's who of the nation. When a member dies, a spot opens. It can take up to 10 years to become a member. Each year, some 30 men are chosen as "first-time" guests and labeled "Mavericks." "Rancheros Vistadores membership is the experience of a lifetime," Dr. Bert Johnson said in an interview in 2014.

Walt Disney rode his horse Minnie Mouse as a guest in the 1930s. Clark Gable joined the ride in 1939. Ronald Reagan rode in the 1970s. Richard Nixon and former Secretary of State George Shultz also joined the ride.

A blessing from the local parish priest in Santa Ynez marks the ride's beginning. Riders then set off on the 20-mile journey to the 16 camps lining Lake Cachuma, where the week of festivities takes place.

Jack's first ride was in 1972. He belongs to the 4-Qs, the largest camp. Each camp is unique with a signature brand. Barbecue, whiskey and stories are shared. Rancheros compete in rodeo events and racetrack competitions.

Jack's 4-Q camp was different from his friend Dr. Bert Johnson's Los Vigilante Camp. "My camp was a camp of gentlemen," Jack joked. "We've got cattlemen, ranchers and just regular people. Johnson's camp has got a bunch of professional team ropers—that's all they've got. To be in his camp, you've got to have a hat size of 8 ½, a collar of 17, a U.S. Team Roping Championship...and an IQ of 30."

"I never made a lot of money riding horses," Jack recalled in an interview in 2016. "But being a cowboy has opened up doors for me. It's provided me the opportunity to meet some of the most wonderful people in the world. I've sat around campfires with some of the richest, most powerful people in the world, and had them tell me they wished they could have led the life I've lived."

After being elected president, Ronald Reagan planned to attend the Rancheros Vistadores opening parade. Each camp creates a float for the parade. Competition runs high. A lot of pride and planning goes into the floats.

A meeting was held to discuss Reagan's security. Jack and Harley May joined. It was agreed: No funny business, no throwing anything at the president or into the crowd. If they did, they'd be kicked out. Jack and May were to tell the other members.

Secret Service agents, outfitted as cowboys, arrived with Reagan. Camouflaged snipers staked out the hills.

Palm Springs Mayor, Frank Bogart, was announcing the parade. Bogart, often the target of 4-Qs pranks, didn't like Jack's camp. One year, the 4-Qs rigged a spigot over the announcer's box. As he announced the floats, the 4-Qs soaked him with water. They cooked up a prank every year.

The parade began. Reagan joined Bill Clark's stagecoach. The coach circled the arena. Then, Reagan retired to the bleachers to watch.

Bogart introduced each camp as their float entered the arena. The Rancheros in the stands clapped and cried out to their fellow campmates.

The 4-Qs were last. Dressed as Franciscan monks, they quietly entered the arena with an elephant trailing behind.

Wrestling the World

They circled the arena and stopped in front of the announcer's box. As the crowd watched, a cowboy ran out with a five-gallon bucket. The elephant dropped his trunk into the bucket, drank the water, then blew it all over Bogart. The crowd roared with laughter. Bogart didn't. He was furious.

The 4-Qs were reprimanded. "But we didn't douse anyone with water!" they protested. "The elephant did it!"

Vistadores Maverick, country western singer, National Football League Super Bowl VII and XIV champion and coach, Jeff Severson and a few other 4-Q members aimed their pranks at Jack.

Jack liked to sing with a band, but not in front of large audiences. The men hung posters announcing that Jack and country legend Dolly Parton would perform "Little Joe the Wrangler" at the 4-Q campsite.

Jack saw the posters. The camp teased him about singing. Jack didn't want to. He hoped most of the camp wouldn't show up.

Band members were setting up their gear and the Rancheros brought in dry ice for special effects. Friends provided Jack with a fringed shirt and apricot scarf.

Jack decided to ham it up. He had bodyguards escort him to the stage. Sporting sunglasses, Jack entered the camp as the crowd chanted, "Roddy, Roddy, Roddy!" Fans lunged toward him, only to be rebuffed by the bodyguards.

Severson introduced him and Jack took the stage and sang "Little Joe the Wrangler." The crowd went wild. Dolly never showed.

In 1974, Jack and the Rancheros sat around drinking and telling stories. The conversation turned into a steer wrestling challenge between Jack and stock contractor Mike Cervi of Sterling, Colorado.

Dr. Bert Johnson remembered the challenge in a 2015 interview. The match was set for the following day. Word spread. Bets were covered. Jack and Cervi would wrestle five steers each. Jack spotted Cervi six seconds, with a 60-second time limit before the crew would shut the gate. The brahmas "had been roped a lot and were unusually strong," Jack recalled.

Jack went first, on a friend's horse. "Since he was a roping horse," Jack said, "he wasn't used to running by the steer. I kept trying to get him alongside so that I could get down, but the horse wouldn't move on up. The back of the arena was coming up at what felt like a hundred miles an hour and I knew I had to do something." Jack leapt out over the steer's head, barely touching the horns.

They both hit the metal gate bars. "I was on his head and not in a dogging position when he hit the gate and I broke my back and a few ribs," Jack remembered.

Johnson heard Jack's ribs break. He ran over to see how badly he was hurt.

Jack got up, took a shallow breath and exhaled in excruciating pain. He looked around the arena and saw everyone who'd bet good money on him. He didn't want to let them down.

Johnson had taped up his ribs and Jack chose another horse for the second run. He stood gripping the gate and watched Cervi win Round 1.

The second run Jack rode the larger, harder-running roping horse alongside the steer, leapt and grabbed the steer by the horns; so far everything had gone smoothly. Then the horse unexpectedly dashed right instead of left and made a U-turn in front of the steer. The horse, steer and Jack collided and tumbled end over end. The 600-pound steer landed on Jack. Onlookers hushed as the second wreck played out. Jack lay there a moment. He knew whatever had broken in his first wreck was worse after this one. With help, he got up from the dirt and made it to the edge of the arena.

Cervi took his second run. He wrestled the steer down. He was up two out of five.

Jack took a long draw of whiskey and got back up on a third horse. Just as he was fixing to grab the steers' horns, the hazer pushed the steer into Jack and its horn plunged into Jack's chest.

"That was it," Jack said. "I had to quit after that."

Wrestling the World

That night Rancho Mission Viejo ranch manager, Gilbert Aguirre threw a tequila and taco party for the Rancheros. The tequila didn't stop the pain, but Jack did his best to drown it.

Bob Hope was entertaining the Rancheros that night in the arena. Jack, Cotton Rosser, Phil Stadtler and Jack Sparrowk made their way down to the show. Upon arriving Jack collapsed in pain. They group took him back to his tent to rest.

Early the next morning, Jack woke up in agony. He packed and started the 270-mile drive back to San Jose, using his left foot on the gas and leaning back into the driver's door to ward off the pain.

"After I had gone about 100 miles, I started feeling as though I couldn't breathe. The tape Dr. Johnson had wrapped around me was constricting my lungs. I stopped and got a knife and cut the tape and pulled it off. By the time I got home, I was a basket case. I could hardly walk," he recalled. "Call the doctor!" he shouted to his wife Julie when he walked into his house.

The next day, an orthopedic surgeon found broken ribs and vertebrae. Jack needed a laminectomy to enlarge his spinal canal and relieve pressure on the cord. Jack underwent surgery three days later. "I told the doctor I wanted to ride again…that I would do anything he said to do, if I could just ride a horse again. He had me up walking an hour after the operation. Three days later I was swimming. Three weeks later, I rode a horse."

Rumors circulated throughout the rodeo community that Jack had suffered a debilitating injury. One cowboy said, "I saw Roddy last month and he's in such bad shape that he can't even straighten up. He'll never be any good again."

Jack spent 12 months in physical therapy and made a full recovery.

"I was reluctant to do any bulldogging. I wanted to try it, but I was scared. I was scared that I wouldn't be able to do it and, if that was the case, I didn't want to know the truth. But one day a reporter from the San Jose Mercury News was doing a story on me and he said he would give anything to get a picture of me in action."

He thought for a few seconds and said: "Get your camera ready. We're going to run a steer." He asked a 14-year-old ranch hand, "You ever haze a steer before? Well, you're going to today."

Jack mounted his horse, the chute opened and "I threw it in a little over three seconds and everything felt good. My timing was good, and it didn't hurt. Just before I got down (on him) I had the most fear I'd ever had about bulldogging. Then, it was over, and I knew I could do it."

His rodeo life wasn't over.

By September, he'd entered the San Jose Rodeo. "I missed a steer but didn't get hurt." The next week he competed in Watsonville and threw a steer in five seconds. He split fourth with another cowboy and earned a $64 check.

"That check was the biggest check of my entire career, because it proved to me that I could bulldog and win again. I always want to stay in rodeo in some capacity. It's my sport. I want to compete as long as I'm able to enjoy it," he said.

At the end of the year at the National Finals in Oklahoma City, Jack was honored with the annual Rodeo Man of the Year Award. Fans and friends watched him accept. Jack was back.

After seven years, Jack made the final payment; the three bars were paid off. He was out of debt and owned the bars.

After making that last payment, Jack and John drove to each bar and Jack bought the house a round. At each bar, he'd announced, "I bought this bar free and clear from my dad. He didn't give it to me." He held up the payment ledger, struck a match and set it afire.

"It was the proudest day of my life," Jack recalled in 2015.

He kept a copy of each payment schedule for proof of payment.

From left, Rancheros Vistadores members: Tony Costa Jr., Jack Roddy, Jack Cooke and Clarence Minetti standing.

Rancheros Vistadores, 4-Q camp members, 1994.

1970 Golden State Rodeo Champion Steer Wrestler - Lucky Lager Award.

Katie Cooney

Jack Roddy - Rodeo Man of the Year 1974, at the National Finals Rodeo in Oklahoma City, Oklahoma. Photo credit: Foxie Photo.

1972 Champion Steer Wrestler Cow Palace Rodeo buckle.

1973 Chowchilla Western Stampede Champion Bull Dogger buckle.

Rancheros Vistadores Team Penning buckle.

Chapter 13

'Hold on!'

What Jack did next surprised some. Jack sold the bars. The cattle business called to him; he'd had enough of bars. "I was good at the bar business," he said. "Good inventory control and my dad taught me well, but I didn't like it. I don't like dealing with people like that. I always liked the cattle business, with its family time and straightforward outdoor work."

Before going into the cattle business, he needed more capital. So, he focused on another financial venture—building a shopping center on property his dad owned in East San Jose.

His dad wanted $87,000 for five lots, paid over five years. Jack borrowed $150,000 to build the center and his dad took a loan to invest in it.

The lots weren't zoned for commercial buildings and Jack needed the zoning changed. So, he invited the City Council to the Fireman's Rodeo and had each member participate on horseback in the festivities.

When he approached the council about rezoning the land, he was on a first-name basis with them all. They unanimously approved the development and rezoned the acreage. Jack sold the center the next year, 1976, and the next year bought Roddy Ranch with the profit.

Rodeo champ and Professional Rodeo Cowboys Association (PRCA) president Dale Smith had called Jack shortly after he sold the bars and built the center and asked, "Do you want to buy a ranch with me?"

Katie Cooney

"Where at?"

"Antioch."

Partnering with an old friend, a childhood hero and mentor sparked his interest. Jack flew north to check the land. He didn't know the property lines, but the area looked good—low, rolling hill country perfect for cattle. He called Smith back: "Just bring your check and I'll meet you here with mine tomorrow."

John's land-buying advice: Find out where they sell it by the square foot a couple miles down the road and compare the price. Make sure the land isn't on the side of a mountain.

Jack and Smith bought 2,156 acres just south of Antioch, in Brentwood. It was a monumental moment. He moved to the ranch and started his new cattle company. Smith was the best partner he'd ever know, Jack recalled; a knowledgeable cattleman, honest and a good cowboy and friend. "Equal partners, we were equal partners," Jack recalled. Smith would visit Roddy Ranch two or three times a year; otherwise, Jack was on his own. He liked that.

Friend and fellow cowboy, Cotton Rosser and his Flying U Rodeo produced a rodeo in Fairfield, close to Brentwood each year. Johnny wanted to take the plane and see the rodeo.

Jack brought the Cessna to Antioch when he bought the ranch but hadn't flown in six months. Rosser told him he flew into Travis Air Force Base when he produced Fairfield's rodeo. Jack decided to fly in with Johnny, and land at Travis. From there they could catch a cab to the rodeo.

The skies were crystal clear on takeoff. Jack knew Travis was a restricted flying zone, but also knew Rosser used it. So—no problem, he figured.

On approach, he radioed Travis tower: "Cessna -----, coming in for a landing."

He put it down with textbook precision. But before he'd stopped, a brigade of trucks mounted with machine guns screamed across the runway…something obviously wasn't right, and Johnny was petrified.

Military Police (MP) surrounded the plane and peppered Jack with questions.

"What are you doing here?"

"I've come to the rodeo," Jack shouted out the window.

"You'll come with us!" they demanded. Jack taxied to a hangar and was marched into an interrogation room.

"Don't you know this is a federal base?" an MP shouted.

"Cotton Rosser used to land here," Jack replied.

But the MP's couldn't comprehend why a cowboy would set down a light plane at a fully operational, protected military base. They kept grilling him.

Finally, they told him a private airstrip sat five miles away. That's where Rosser landed. Jack was in a mess. Johnny shook with fright. Jack suggested a truce.

"Look, the rodeo starts in another hour. You've got my plane. Let us go to the rodeo and I'll come back."

The MP's saw Jack and Johnny were no threat. After a little more questioning, they impounded the plane and told Jack to return to fly out after the rodeo.

Jack and Johnny met up with Rosser at the rodeo. Rosser introduced them to a general and two colonels playing cowboy. Jack didn't mention the mess at Travis.

The rodeo kicked off with wild cow milking. The event dates back to the late 1920s, first recorded at Cheyenne's Frontier Days. Four teams of three men compete to get a drop of milk from a spooky cow into a soda bottle and run it across the finish line. The first team across wins—mostly bragging rights.

The four milking teams at Fairfield were from the military; Marines, Navy, Air Force and Army. The brass Jack had just met were the Air Force team. They were older than the other servicemen, but up for the challenge.

But none of the Air Force bigwigs knew anything about milking a wild cow. So, Jack got them down in front of the chutes and gave detailed descriptions and directions.

He finally told them the secret to winning: "General, just before it starts, walk over to the ice cream stand and get yourself a scoop of vanilla. Take a mouthful and go back to the chutes and wait for the gun. Then, run on into the arena, get your head down real close to that cow and spit the melted ice cream into the bottle. Then run like hell to the finish line."

The general had enjoyed a few drinks and didn't get the timing quite right. He walked over and ordered his ice cream a full 30 minutes before the contest. By the time he and his team were standing at the chutes waiting for the starting gun, vanilla ice cream was running from both sides of his mouth.

He still had enough in his mouth to win. But after they'd led the haltered mama from the chute and held her so he could butt up to her flank and pull his sleight-of-mouth, she pulled back. He spit the remaining ice cream down his shirt as the crowd cheered.

"Goddammit, now you've gotta milk her!" Jack shouted at him.

The general amazed Jack by getting a drop of milk from her udder into the bottle. He sprinted for the finish line like an eager young cowboy. The general's team took a respectable second place, a real accomplishment considering their ages, their lack of experience and the load of liquor they were packing.

They thanked Jack for his inside instructions and sideline coaching. The general invited Jack and his family back to the base.

"Well, you might do me a favor," Jack told him.

Jack explained his problem and the general made a call. At the end of the day, he gave Jack and Johnny a jeep ride back to the base, right to their plane. They shook hands and Johnny and Jack flew home, laughing about the ice cream dribbling from the general's mouth.

Jack continued to fly despite his many mishaps and close calls. But, a brush with death on the flight home from a Cedarville cutting-horse show in 1977 finally persuaded Jack to hang up his wings. He was flying Dave McGregor and Mike Compili back home and tried to land at Sparrowk's ranch in Clements.

The plane had passed its annual inspection two weeks before, but one brake failed on landing. Jack hollered, "Hang on!" and stuffed the plane in a gully. The plane bounced hard down the gully, across a field and landed upright. Once Jack knew they were OK, he crawled out. McGregor and Compili sat in shock.

"Joe, you got a fence tool?" Jack shouted at Compili. The propeller had caught in a fence wire.

Jack freed the prop, taxied to the runway and parked it.

A week later, Jack drove to pick up the plane. He brought a pilot friend and asked if he'd done the right thing stuffing the plane in the gully. The pilot confirmed Jack had done it right. Had he tried to pull the plane back up, he'd have crashed into a bank of trees and died.

"I needed to quit," he said. "I was too gutsy." He sold the plane soon after.

After 16 years on the RCA and PRCA boards of directors, Jack resigned at the 1978 Las Vegas meeting. He'd been instrumental in elevating rodeo to a multi-million-dollar sport.

Jack Roddy steer wrestling in Santa Maria, 1976.

Jack Roddy steer wrestling at the Salinas Rodeo, 1978.

Jack Roddy - San Jose, California.

Chapter 14

'I fought the federal government and beat 'em. I fought this country one time and beat 'em. I fought the city here and beat 'em. It was you that taught me how to do that.'

In the mid-'70s, a group of businesspeople approached PRCA President Dale Smith, Jack and the board to build a national rodeo hall of fame in Colorado Springs, Colorado.

The National Cowboy & Western Heritage Museum in Oklahoma City was a well-established institution that promoted, recognized and preserved the American West. A hall celebrating professional rodeo and its champions in Colorado Springs made sense; the PRCA was headquartered in Denver at that time.

Jack and Smith decided to explore the possibility. They surveyed the 10 acres near the Garden of the Gods and the airport. They agreed the location was great.

Fundraising commenced across the country: Ropings, events, barbecues, private solicitations and concerts by country musician Red Steagall and others. Cowboys, performers, fans and supporters joined forces to raise $1 million for the land and hall.

The Museum of the American Cowboy and ProRodeo Hall of Fame opened in August 1979 as an "educational and entertaining museum designed to preserve the legacy of the cowboy contests, the heritage and culture of those original competitors and the champions of the past, present and future," according to the ProRodeo Hall of Fame.

The hall has inducted 250 men, women and animals since its opening. Inductees must have retired and won at least one world championship. Other inductees include individuals who have promoted and expanded the sport of rodeo, including U.S. Secretary of Commerce Malcolm Baldrige, inducted in 1988.

Jack was inducted in 1979 at age 42, along with steer wrestlers Hugh Bennett, James Bynum, Roy Duvall, John W. Jones Sr., Harley May and Homer Pettigrew. Champions showcase their memorabilia, saddles, buckles and trophies in the Hall.

Retired livestock inductees live at the museum for visitors to see. Oscar the Bull retired and was inducted in 1979's inaugural class. He spent his final, leisurely years on the property and died there in 1983. In 2013 and 2018, Oscar also was inducted into the Salinas Rodeo and Bull Riding Halls of Fame.

Jack and Julie divorced, and Jack swore off marrying again. Two marriages had ended in divorce and he wasn't interested in dating seriously. Friend Tony Costa encouraged Jack to court Donna Hamm, the general manager at Fisco Western Wear in Tracy, California, a ranch-supply store. Jack knew her as a talented horseback rodeo rider.

"You need to talk to her," Tony pressured Jack.

Hamm was born and raised in the Sebastopol area of Marin County. Recently divorced, Donna needed a place to live. She rented a room from an older woman in the Brentwood area, but needed a place to board her horse and keep her dog.

Jack owned rentals in San Jose. Friends encouraged her to call him.

She called. They visited some ranches in the highlands of San Jose. Jack said, "Look, these houses aren't good for you. Let me see if I can find you something better."

They started dating and fell in love. Donna moved in.

She continued working at Fisco's and Jack ran the ranch. She was a real "people person," Jack liked to say. Ranchers would drive for miles just for a chance to talk with her. Donna is 5 feet, 10 inches with arresting hazel eyes and blond hair. Personable and kind, she is a true beauty. And she could also rope and ride with the best of them.

Ann and John continued living on Sierra Ranch. Without the bars, John was home and doing odd jobs around the property. Ann told Jack that John was becoming more and more forgetful. It was getting difficult to care for him.

Jack suggested they move to Roddy Ranch and lease Sierra Ranch. Jack bought his mom a nice trailer he put on the property. She could have her privacy and be nearby. John went to live in a convalescent home in Brentwood.

Cattlemen struggled in the 1980s. Demand for beef waned as Americans ate more chicken, turkey, fish and pork. Competing industries vied for consumer dollars.

The Dairy Production Stabilization Act of 1983 paid subsidies to dairy farmers if they reduced their output by 5 to 30 percent of their annual base. That nearly broke the American cattle industry. The voluntary program allowed milk producers to reduce their output with no financial repercussions and paid them if they culled their herds of the highest-producing cows.

When the act was introduced, the ratio of beef to dairy cows stood at 10 to one—some 110 million beef cows to 10 million dairy cows. To avoid flooding the beef market with dairy cows and creating a surplus, the government decided to impose an "orderly market," with the support of the California Cattlemen and National Cattlemen Associations.

That "orderly" market would cull the hyper-producing dairy cows over an 18-month period, trying to ensure the beef industry would not lose millions of dollars when a surge of beef hit the market, thus protecting the cattlemen and their industry from going broke. It might have worked. But it never happened. During a July 2018 interview, Jack said, "the 'orderly market' just didn't happen. Why? I don't know."

In April, cows stop feeding on grass and cattlemen shipped them to feedlots. That year, in a week's time, dairy cattle flooded stockyards across the country and the price of beef dropped 12 cents per pound. The beef market collapsed. Jack had 4,000 head between Clements, Brentwood and San Jose. When the market dropped, he lost $125 per head, more than half-million dollars.

That April, Jack shipped 4,000 head to a feedlot and waited for the market to recover. Desperate, others sold for whatever they could get. Some went broke. There are no figures on how much cattlemen lost, or damages incurred from the Dairy Diversion Program, but in the end, taxpayers would foot the bill. Jack said the Dairy Diversion Program "cost taxpayers two-and-a-half billion dollars."

Cattlemen across the country were losing just as much as Jack or more. Ranchers rarely own their land outright, so if they didn't meet their financial obligations the bank would step in and they'd be out of business.

John Lacey, president of the California Cattlemen's Association and an old college friend of Jack's, called. He told Jack dairy cows were being dumped on the market and cattlemen needed help. He asked Jack to call Malcolm Baldrige in Washington, D.C., for help.

Jack told Baldrige the diversion was wreaking havoc on the beef market. Baldrige knew nothing about it. He told Jack to fly to Washington and they'd discuss it. Five minutes later, the Agriculture Secretary Richard Lyng called Jack.

"I don't know what the heck you guys are doing," Jack told him, "but you're breaking the West. I lost a half-million dollars overnight."

That Friday, Jack and cattleman Jack Sparrowk flew to Washington. Baldrige picked them up in his old Jeep Wagoneer—still a cowboy at heart.

Over the weekend, they roped in Virginia as Jack filled him in about the Dairy Diversion disaster. Baldrige suggested he speak to the folks in the Capitol. He told Jack to wear his jeans, boots and a cowboy hat.

Monday morning in May, Jack accompanied Baldrige to the Herbert C. Hoover Building, headquarters of the Commerce Department on Constitution Avenue. Sparrowk had to fly home because his son was in a car accident.

Jack and Baldrige met with White House counsel. The attorney advised Baldrige to recuse himself from Diversion program action; Baldrige owned a ranch in New Mexico, a conflict of interest. Further, he was an advisor to the ProRodeo Cowboy

Wrestling the World

Association directors. He agreed, but guided Jack on what to do next. He gave Jack a list of names, nicknames, and four-digit internal-government phone numbers. Over two days, Jack called every politician on the list, explaining the cattlemen's situation and how the flood of dairy cows was breaking them.

Months later, in August, the beef market stabilized. Politicians agreed to send a considerable quantity of the culled beef to U.S. Armed Forces overseas and 400,000 dairy cows to Brazil. Cattlemen rejoiced.

In July and August 1983, Jack moved his 4,000 head of cattle from the feedlot to the sales lot. He survived the Great Dairy Diversion Disaster.

With the disaster behind him, Jack was ready for a little fun with childhood friend and roping partner, Jack Cooke. Cooke, who would retire from the Hearst Corporation in 1998, was president of the Rancheros Vistadores, president of the Grand National Cow Palace in San Francisco and board president of the National Cowboy Hall of Fame.

In 1983, Cooke and his wife Phoebe Hearst dined with Queen Elizabeth on the royal yacht Britannia in San Francisco Bay. Weeks later, Cooke invited Jack to Tombstone, Arizona, to check out a gold mine he'd bought. Jack jumped at the chance.

The next day, they had a drink in Tombstone. Cooke told Jack about the dinner with Queen Elizabeth and Prince Philip. Cooke spoke of the fanfare and the city's elite.

Jack said he was interested in buying some cattle from Mexico. He suggested they drive to Douglas on the border and check out the market.

At the Douglas Hotel they ran into Phil Stadtler, Jack's old friend and leading cattleman who imported Mexican steers. They went for drinks and heard what Stadtler was up to.

Stadtler's friend Ruben Morales joined the three for drinks. Ruben invited them to dinner just over the border. They drained their glasses and headed for the restaurant.

They loaded into "Lupe," Stadtler's old Oldsmobile "trading car" he kept in Mexico:

Katie Cooney

Torn upholstery, bullet holes in the side panels—it was a mess.

South of the border, Stadtler did business in Lupe.

The restaurant catered to wealthy patrons. Mexican cattlemen greeted Stadtler, calling him "Patron" out of respect for his business savvy. Stadtler owned more than 250,000 head—one of the biggest players in the business. The men spoke to Stadtler about overthrowing the Mexican government after their cattle were confiscated. Stadtler's influence impressed Jack.

At one in the morning, Stadtler jumped up and yelled, "Let's go to Club Aristocrat!"

They entered the lonesome club and found an overweight woman slumped over the bar. The men ordered a round of drinks. Stadtler sat next to the woman, Jack recalled and "grabbed her ass. She let out a war hoop."

Roddy and Cooke laughed themselves silly.

Stadtler popped out his glass eye and dropped it in his shot glass. The woman screamed.

"Jack let's get out of here," Cooke said to Jack.

"No way. We're having fun."

"Look around, you dumb son of a gun."

Three men on the right...three men on the left. Sunglasses and black leather jackets. They looked like they meant business.

"Let's get out of here!" Jack poked Stadtler.

Outnumbered, they paid and left.

Heading back to the border, Jack turned to Cooke and laughed, "You're the most versatile man I know. Three weeks ago, you were having dinner with the Queen of

Wrestling the World

England on the Britannia in San Francisco Bay, and tonight you were in a Mexican whorehouse with Stadtler and me."

"And I had more fun with you and Stadtler!" Cooke said, laughing.

Cooke's wife and Hearst heiress, Phoebe, loved the story. "It put a down-to-earth face on her husband, which is exactly the kind of man he was," Jack recalled.

In May 1983, Jack was shipping cattle in San Jose when his sister Nancy called and told him she'd found their mother dead in her home. At 76 years old, Ann had suffered a fatal heart attack.

Jack eulogized her simply in 2018: "She was a kind, loving mother."

Before John passed away the following year, in May 1984, Jack told him, "I fought the federal government and beat 'em. I fought this country one time and beat 'em. I fought the city here and beat 'em. It was you that taught me how to do that."

The poverty John had endured as a child had haunted him all his life. He achieved the American Dream but found it difficult to shake the ghosts. The fight inside him made him successful in business, but it also fueled the competitive, combative relationship with his son Jack. He wouldn't spoil his children, especially Jack. They had no special privileges and had to earn their own success, as he had.

Jack believed his dad's tough discipline made him who he was. "He made me by not being easy on me. He made it tough," Jack said.

At the invitation of Jack and the California Cattlemen's Association Baldrige flew to California for a weekend of roping, barbecuing and gratitude for his help shutting down the Dairy Diversion Program.

The day began with a team roping competition. Baldrige and Sparrowk were first up. Sparrowk roped the steer's head as Baldrige laid a loop around the heels. Baldrige dallied his rope around the saddle horn; the horse flipped straight over backward and landed on top of him.

Jack! Your friend's down!" a reporter yelled.

Jack raced across the arena to Baldrige. He wasn't breathing.

"Call Muir Hospital! We need to get him out of here!" Jack hollered.

A helicopter flew Baldrige to John Muir in Walnut Creek. He was rushed into surgery and died on the table 90 minutes later of a torn aorta.

President Reagan, who knew Jack from their time at Rancheros Vistadores, called and asked Jack to accompany the body back to Washington aboard Air Force One. He agreed.

The funeral was in Washington Cathedral. Cowboys and politicians gathered to remember their friend and colleague. Baldrige was buried in North Cemetery in Woodbury, Connecticut.

For several months, a burden of grief bore Jack down. He didn't speak of Baldrige's death.

Speculation on how Baldrige died ensued. Baldrige had used a tie-down that linked the horse's nose to its breast collar, giving the horse something to pull against in tight turns and control its head. The rigging may have caused the horse to rear back and jump over backward. And one onlooker said he'd seen a strange look cross Baldrige's face when he dallied, then jerked back on the reins unusually hard, causing the horse to flip backward; perhaps he had a heart attack before the fall.

The coroner reported Baldrige died of cardiac arrest caused by extensive bleeding in the abdomen.

The cattlemen and cowboys nominated Baldrige for the ProRodeo Hall of Fame and asked Jack to accept the award on his behalf. In 1988, Jack accepted the award at the Hall of Fame.

Baldrige's philosophy was, "Success is finding something you really like to do and caring enough about it to do it well…(and) sticking your neck out if you're sure you're right and getting lucky."

In five years, Jack lost both his mom and dad and his dearest friend and roping partner Malcolm Baldrige. He loved them all, but knew life went on.

In 1988, Jack married again. He'd vowed a decade earlier he wouldn't, but Donna was different. She adored him. She worked the cattle as hard as he did and could keep up with him. They understood one another.

Jack quietly planned to marry her before a steer-roping event at the ranch. He wanted something simple and knew Donna did too.

Jack invited Alan Keller, Jack Cooke and Phoebe Hearst as witnesses. They arrived at 9 a.m. and brought a judge. As the cattlemen arrived, Jack pulled Donna aside and said, "Come on."

Jack led her to the oak in the backyard, where a small group gathered. She understood.

Judge Walker said his words, they said theirs, and it was done. They were married.

They announced their union at the arena. Everyone cheered and congratulated them. A good and happy day ended in a party. "And that's how we celebrated our wedding," Jack remembered.

Donna and Jack recently celebrated their 31st wedding anniversary.

Married life was good and so was the cattle business. Jack spent his days on horseback checking on the steers and mending fences. He'd come a long way from the bar business.

Thirteen years after leaving the Gill Ranch, Jack got a call from a Gilroy brand inspector. He'd found two steers with the Roddy brand on them in a local processing shop. The inspector wanted to know if Jack knew about them.

"They're Gill cattle," Jack said.

Katie Cooney

Wild cattle wandered onto the Gill from Coe State Park. But these two steers were at least 15 years old, branded when Jack leased and managed the Gill.

"Where'd you uncover them?" Jack asked.

"A rancher near the Gill."

"Is he a cattle rancher?"

"No, he's a young guy, but he's kind of a decent kind of a guy, said they were on his ranch."

"That's not true. They were in Coe Park."

"One of them had a beautiful head. He's having one of the heads mounted."

"Well, is this rancher a cowboy?"

"No, he can hardly swing a rope."

"Whoa. Something wrong here," Jack said.

Jack made some calls himself, first to the young rancher.

"I'm Jack Roddy. I heard you have a couple of my steers."

"Well, they were on my ranch."

"Listen, do me a favor. Don't lie to me. I know the steers were in Coe Park. Them big steers don't jump fences, number one. I understand you can't rope. Who was with you?"

The rancher provided the name of his accomplice.

"That name doesn't ring a bell." Jack said. "Look. I want that head. I hear you're having it mounted."

Wrestling the World

"Yes, I am."

"OK, when will it be done?"

"First of July."

"Ok, bring it to Salinas Rodeo, free and clear. OK?"

Jack attended the Salinas Rodeo: No rancher, no head. Jack called again.

"Where's my head?"

"It's coming."

"Christmas is coming. Where's my head?"

"I'll have it in two weeks."

Two weeks passed. No word, no head.

Jack called the Northern District State Inspector General and asked him to track down the accomplice. The Inspector found him at the Oregon border. The next week Jack got a call from the rancher.

"We need to talk," he said.

"You'd better hurry up. You're gonna be in real trouble with the State Inspector, because you lied to me."

"We'll meet you tomorrow at your ranch."

The rancher and cowboy arrived at the ranch the next morning. Jack invited a friend to sit in on the conversation. Jack invited the cowboy into the house. The rancher remained on the porch.

"Jack, you remember me?"

Katie Cooney

"No."

"I used to rodeo. You signed for my PRCA card. I was a bronc rider."

"I do remember you now."

The cowboy was a nice young kid and one hell of a cowboy, as Jack remembered.

"How'd you get those steers?"

"Well, they were in Coe Park. I found the one, roped him and tied him to a tree. Then I found the other one, roped him and tied him to another tree."

The rancher paced on the front porch. Jack went out to speak to him.

"You're making a big deal out of this," he told Jack.

"Come in the house. I want to tell you something."

"What do you want to do?"

"I'll tell you what I want you to do. I want you to write me a check for $11,000."

"For what?" he laughed.

"Let me tell you. This cowboy, he's the Head Brand Inspector for Northern California. He heard every word you and the cowboy said. That's cattle rustling, which is grand theft in California, with a three-year maximum prison term. Any stolen cattle are paid for at three or four times their value; so, you add 2,800 pounds, plus 2,600 pounds, times 72 cents a pound, and write me a check, or you're going to San Quentin."

The rancher crumbled. He begged Jack to drop the whole thing. But the runaround had gotten Jack sore. He wasn't going to let him off that easy. He lectured him for 20 minutes and finally said, "Listen, If you hadn't lied to me this wouldn't have happened. But I want that head. You write me a check today for $1,000 and have that head on my doorstep tomorrow morning. Clear?"

Wrestling the World

The rancher wrote the check and delivered the mounted head early the next morning and left.

The old steer now watches over the Roddy living room.

Jack still itched to compete. "A cowboy misses his friends and the thrill of competition," Jack told a writer in 1992.

The Senior ProRodeo Tour commenced in 1979; 60 sanctioned rodeos now occur annually. Participants must be over the age of 40 and belong to the National Senior ProRodeo Association. Contestants compete in bareback riding, barrel racing, bull riding, tie-down roping, ribbon roping, saddle-bronc riding, team roping, ladie's and men's breakaway and steer wrestling.

Friend Brent Gilbert asked Jack to produce a senior rodeo at the Contra Costa State Fair in Antioch in 1991. Jack and Gilbert agreed to underwrite the Senior Finals for three years. Former champs and amateurs alike welcomed the chance to compete once again.

Jack joined the senior circuit in 1991. He felt he could still compete with the younger cowboys.

Jack decided he wanted to win the 1991 National Senior ProRodeo Steer Wrestling Championship.

At 54, Jack weighed 240 pounds. He had to get in shape. He ran to the top of the ridge behind the ranch every morning. The first morning took him 30 minutes; he was winded when he reached the top. The next day, he did it again. Each day he got a little faster. At the Senior Finals he weighed in at 215 pounds.

Jack entered the bulldogging event at the National Senior ProRodeo Finals in 1991 and captured the Steer Wrestling World Championship.

Jack told Donna he was going for the '92 title. He thought he could be lucky—twice.

Each year, more than 1,500 association members competed across the West and

Katie Cooney

Canada to qualify for the Senior Finals. The contestants were grouped by age, 40 to 50, and 50 and up. In team roping, the age category extended to 60 and older. Cowboys and cowgirls, at 70 and 80, were competing in the less-punishing team and calf roping events.

When Jack reached the Senior Finals in Reno that November, he'd roped in 10 rodeos and placed in steer wrestling.

At the finals, Jack wrestled his steer in 4 seconds flat. He won the Steer Wrestling World Championship in 1992.

From left, Jack Roddy, Dale Smith, Dave Stout and Larry Dawson. ProRodeo Hall of Fame champions 1980. Photo credit: Theodore L. Goebe

Jack Roddy steer wrestling in Oakdale, CA in 1980.
Photo credit: Barbara Allen.

From left, Jack Cooke, Jack Roddy and Phoebe Hearst.

From left, Malcolm Baldrige and Jack Roddy steer roping.
Photo credit: Foxie photo.

1990 Malcolm "Mac" Baldrige Memorial Roping Champion buckle.

Donna and Jack Roddy.

Jack and Donna Roddy at Roddy Ranch arena.

Jack Roddy steer wrestling at the National Old Timers Rodeo Association (NOTRA) at Wood Mountain, Saskatchewan, Canada, 1991.
Photo credit: Jan Spencer.

Jack Roddy steer wrestling, 1992. Photo credit: Jan Spencer.

From left, Canadian cowboy Tom Bailey and American cowboy Jack Roddy, National Old Timers Rodeo Association Steer Wrestling Champions in 1992. Photo credit: Jan Spencer.

1992 Seniors ProRodeo NOTRA
Worlds Champion Steer Wrestler buckle.

1992 National Senior Pro Rodeo Finals.

1992 Chowchilla Stampede Champion Century Header.

1992 NCCHA Reserve Champion Green Novice.

Chapter 15

*'When I speak today, you won't believe what I'm going to tell you...
but I've never been caught in a lie.'*

During the 1990s, Jack played a pivotal role in educating cattlemen on the dangers of eco-terrorism and the groups that were terrorizing their industry. He worked tirelessly to protect livestock, property and the way of life he loved. At times the danger was imminent, but he pushed on. His honest reputation and list of contacts gave him access to agriculture and ranching industry leaders. He saw their way of life and livelihoods were under attack.

During the mid-80's, Jack heard reports of attacks on ranches and farms; cutting barbed wire fences, shooting cattle and burning down cattle auction barns. Livestock were killed, as well. He also heard talk of ending public-land leases to ranchers for grazing cattle.

Jack attended a meeting in the East Bay, where a mix of ranchers, cattlemen and "young long-haired hippies" attended, Jack recalled. Protesters brandished signs which read "Meat free by '93", "Meat is Murder" and "Cow Free by '93". "I recoiled when I heard all of this," Jack said in a 2015 interview.

Back at home, he called fellow Cal Poly alum John Lacey, president of the California Cattlemen's Association.

"John, I'm hearing a lot of things about hay barns being burned and fences destroyed, and cattle being killed," he said. "It's been blamed on vandals, but these protesters were flying a banner that read 'Earth First!' It really bothered me."

Katie Cooney

Lacey knew Jack had served on the PRCA Animal Care Committee, which worked to ensure the well-being and protection of stock. He asked Jack to lead a new animal-care committee for the California Cattlemen's Association.

"Well, I'll be glad to start the committee," he told Lacey. "I want to fight my way, but I'll start the committee."

Once the committee was organized, he started his own investigation.

A friend mailed Jack Earth First! newspapers and articles regarding vandalism. Jack bought a copy of the Earth First! manual, Ecodefense: A Field Guide to Monkeywrenching, by Bill Haywood (Abzug Press,1993). It provided a step-by-step guide of how to destroy roads, build firebombs and damage heavy equipment.

Jack read the manual and doubled his efforts to alert fellow cattlemen about the threat. Jack financed his fight against eco-terrorists. "I'll never take a dollar from anybody," he said.

Business continued as usual at Roddy Ranch. Jack shipped 600 head of cattle to Dale Smith in Arizona. But soon after, the ranch manager reported 40 dead steers on the side of the road.

"Dale...found all these dead steers. They were all healthy, standing by the roads (then) they found their skulls caved in, no evidence, 40 of them dead," he said.

Jack and Smith called other Arizona stock growers, who said they couldn't understand all the destruction across the country. Miles of fence had been torn up, he learned, barns had been torched, cattle had been shot and the ranchers were at a loss.

Jack had been vociferously public about his findings and opinions about Earth First! and eco-terrorism.

When Friends of Rodeo sent an undercover agent to Los Angeles to meet with an Earth First! group in 1989, the agent discovered Jack's name and address on a list.

Wrestling the World

"There were five names," he recounted. "To kill? I can't tell you that, but our names were batted about within this group of terrorists," said Jack.

Two days after learning his name had been circulated, his first steer was killed at Roddy Ranch. Fourteen more followed. Local sheriff's deputies investigated. The coroner found a .38-caliber bullet in each of the steers' heads. Jack wondered how safe he and Donna were.

A few weeks later, on January 29, 1989, the Schene family's Dixon Livestock Auction House in California burned to the ground in a fire that investigators determined was intentionally set. The damage was estimated as high as $400,000. An anonymous male caller told the Associated Press in Sacramento the fire was the work of Earth First! The caller said they were targeting the livestock industry because of the damage it causes to the environment.

Furthermore, he said they spray painted Earth First! and Agribusiness Kills slogans on the walls of the California Cattlemen's Office in Sacramento. An Earth First! representative denied knowledge of the fire but stated members could be involved.

After the Dixon blaze, Jack was asked to join a Stockton meeting of the California Sales Yard Owners. People were worried; the Dixon fire cut close to home.

Jack spoke in Stockton about what was happening across the state. He told them Earth First! was organized, with members committed to wreak havoc on the cattle industry.

Cal Poly friend Dave Wood managed the Harris Ranch feedlot, a well-known ranch and beef producer in Coalinga. The feedlot tended 120,000 head of cattle. Wood asked Jack to attend a meeting with the FBI and bring all his materials on eco-terrorism. The FBI had heard Harris Ranch was targeted for an attack. Security at the meeting was high. Police helicopters circled above, and the California Highway Patrol watched the roads. Law-enforcement task forces stood by.

"They knew nothing," Jack recalled of his meeting with the FBI.

One of the sheriffs asked the FBI how the Dixon feedlot had been torched. The agents replied they didn't know.

"I know how they did it," Jack said.

"How'd they do it?" the agent smirked.

"Mr. FBI man, they circled the feedlot with gas. They set it on fire. It was burning in 15 minutes. They did $250,000 worth of damage," Jack stated.

"How in the hell do you know?" the FBI agent shouted.

"Mr. FBI man, I can tell you the man who issued that order to burn down the Dixon feedlot. I can tell you where he lives and I can give you his phone number in Tucson, Arizona," Jack said.

Wood told the agents Jack might know more than they did.

"I know far more," Jack interjected.

He walked down the center aisle and dropped his briefcase on the table. He pulled out articles, magazines and clippings he'd collected on eco-terrorism.

Jack and the FBI started working together.

In 1990, Jack spoke at the National Cattlemen's Convention in Dallas. Jack began, "When I speak today, you won't believe what I'm going to tell you. But I've never been caught in a lie. When I get done, make me prove it." He gave an overview of eco-terrorism around the nation. Cattlemen listened in shock. After his talk, they bombarded him with questions, worried about their cattle operations.

The lack of national news coverage concerned Jack. The lack of coverage in the livestock, ranching and cattlemen publications angered him.

Jack continued to speak out to expose eco-terrorists. Jack thought little about his own safety, but worried about Donna. He carried a .44 Magnum and kept another by the front door. An FBI agent advised Jack to stop opening packages delivered to his house and to take them instead to the sheriff's office, where they were inspected. The Roddys didn't open a package for two years. Jack installed electric gates at the ranch and police began patrolling the road.

Beef Today published an article in February 1992 titled Animal Right's Front Line, by reporter Greg Lamp. It outlined the violence and attacks against cattlemen around the country. It highlighted the Dixon Livestock arson, for which Earth First! had claimed responsibility. The group also took credit for an attack on the California Cattlemen's Association headquarters in Sacramento and 60 acts of violence in the state committed since 1984, all in the name of protecting "animal rights."

Jack had spent a decade tracking eco-terrorists and this was the first report in an agriculture publication. Lamp described how terrorists killed animals, while also targeting cattlemen like Jack.

"Ranchers have to realize that they're the 'enemy,'" Lamp quoted Jack. "Activists want to drive us out of business. We've got to be prepared and stay ahead of them."

Another terrorist was high on the FBI wanted list. Unabomber Ted Kaczynski had sent lethal package bombs to animal researchers and academics, killing three and injuring 23 over a 17-year bombing campaign. On September 22, 1995, Kaczynski submitted his 35,000-word "Manifesto" to the New York Times and the Washington Post. Both published the 100-page document, which outlined the ills of modern society and why life proved difficult for ordinary citizens.

Jack read the word "Luddite" in connection with the Unabomber. He recalled Earth First!'s leader was also a self-described "Luddite." Jack's gut told him the Unabomber was an Earth First! member.

Jack called the San Francisco FBI hotline number and spoke to FBI Special Agent Max Noel. "Look, I'm not some nut calling you, I've worked with you guys. I've given you a lot of information on the ranchers and cattlemen who have been attacked. You're going to find out that this Unabomber was a member of Earth First! because he used the word 'Luddite' in the Manifesto."

After a tip from Kaczynski's brother, Special Agent Noel arrested Kaczynski in his cabin in Lincoln, Montana on April 3, 1996.

During the trial, prosecutors presented evidence of communication between Kaczynski and members of Earth First! Kaczynski had used the Earth First! hit list, which Roddy's name was on, to target his bombing victims, according to Rogelio A. Maduro in the EIR National article "Unabomber admits ties to Earth First! Eco-terrorists."

Jack and the cattlemen felt safer with Kaczynski behind bars.

Jack worked for more than a decade in the shadow of the FBI and other law enforcement agencies, uncovering information, raising the red flag and educating ranchers across the West about the threat of eco-terrorism and those dedicated to it. Protecting animals, people and ranch life was his mission and he never let up.

Chapter 16

'The public knew then that there was nobody madder than me about all this fraud.'

After 21 years of running cattle on the ranch, Dale Smith and Jack were strapped for cash and behind on mortgage payments. The instability of the cattle market, increased feed costs and droughts all had pressed on the business. Foreclosure was imminent.

Jack spoke to a friend who'd developed part of his father's Sierra Ranch in San Jose. Jack told him "I don't have the wherewithal to keep this going. The cattle just don't work." The friend introduced Jack to Wayne Pierce, a mortgage banker involved with major developments in San Jose. Maybe Jack and Smith could develop a part of Roddy Ranch to subsidize the business.

A few weeks later, Pierce offered to buy out Smith's stake in the 2,200-acre ranch. Land-rich and cash-strapped, Smith sold Pierce his majority stake in the ranch, a stake that carried with it Jack's reputation as a straight shooter and the allure of his rodeo success. Jack believed he was in good hands with Pierce. He welcomed his new partner and the hope for a financial turnaround. There was no hint of the disaster to come.

As they brainstormed projects, Jack made it clear to Pierce he wanted the hills surrounding the ranch preserved. And he told him any project with his name on it had to be first-class, Jack recalled.

Jack said Pierce told him about the Mare Island golf course he owned in Vallejo, purportedly the oldest course west of the Mississippi. Roddy Ranch would be a perfect place to build a course the men decided. They formed a limited-liability company, with Pierce as managing partner owning 70 percent of the company. Jack hired the club pro and the finance manager, he said, then focused on the struggling cattle business.

In 1998, they broke ground. The course offered vistas of Mount Diablo to the west and the city of Brentwood to the east. The 40-acre ranch remained private, nestled between Mount Diablo and the golf course. Between Empire Mine Road and Balfour Road off Deer Valley Road, they built a new road to the course, Tour Way. The white clubhouse included staff offices, the pro shop and a restaurant. Jack felt secure, he said, with Pierce's oversight, experience, and financial resources.

Jack hired PGA Golf Pro Kevin Fitzgerald from Arizona, then spent months interviewing and hiring staff as the course and clubhouse neared completion.

Roddy Ranch Golf Course opened in late 2000 to immediate success. The 235-acre course became one of the most popular in the East Bay for its picturesque setting, casual club atmosphere, and friendly staff.

The golf course flourished, and Jack enjoyed seeing friends who'd come to play a round; his financial troubles appeared solved.

At the end of each fiscal year, Jack got a report on the financials from Pierce. Everything look above-board: "This was a pretty good deal," he said later.

But as the months passed, Jack found himself spending more time managing day-to-day course operations and less time at the ranch. "I'm up there settling disputes, labor disputes on and on," he said. Pierce "wasn't coming around. I'm starting to get a little tender."

Jack heard rumors the golf course had financial troubles, but said he felt secure with Pierce's financial backing. "He owned a mortgage company in Dublin," Jack recalled, "had a Rolls Royce, fancy clothes and was a smooth-talking guy."

Jack got a call mid-summer of 2001 from his friend, Contra Costa County Sheriff Dick Raney, warning him about "the bonds." Jack had no idea what he was talking about.

Raney told him bonds were being floated against the Ranch. Jack began to suspect Pierce might not be all he'd been cracked up to be.

In 2001, Jack noticed a man at the clubhouse one day.

"Who are you? "Jack asked him.

"I'm your partner," replied David Fitzgerald (no relation to golf pro Kevin Fitzgerald).

"No partner of mine," snapped Jack.

"You understand bonds?" Fitzgerald asked.

"I can't spell bonds," Jack snapped back.

Fitzgerald turned and left.

Two days later, Jack said, a limousine arrived at the Ranch. Fitzgerald handed Jack a thick stack of papers. Jack scanned the first few documents and decided, "Way beyond my pay grade."

Pierce had brought in David Fitzgerald's Pacific Genesis to finance the golf course and a high-end, 1,000-home residential development around it. Between 1998-2000, Pacific Genesis Group sold $35 million in Roddy Ranch tax-free municipal bonds to finance the project. The sale of those homes was supposed to repay investors, the pitch went.

The development of luxury homes depended on county zoning. At the formation of the partnership, part of the ranch land was within the county's urban limit line, so there was the potential of developing the land into luxury homes. The line was redrawn, excluding the ranch. County supervisors had to redraw the line before the homes could be built.

The next time Fitzgerald arrived in his limousine. Jack ran him off.

Jack needed a right-hand man; someone he could trust implicitly. Kevin Fitzgerald, the golf pro, was the man. "Run this course," Jack told Kevin.

Kevin discovered one of the employees and David Fitzgerald had exchanged hundreds of emails. Kevin printed 200 pages of them and showed them to Jack, who was furious.

Jack said he told Pierce the bonds were a phony deal. Jack, Pierce and Fitzgerald met with Jack's friend the city manager of Antioch. He wanted the mess straightened out. The meeting proved useless. Jack told the city manager he thought the bonds were phony.

A couple of months later, Kevin told Jack he was quitting. Pierce was riding him hard and he was fed up. Jack invited Kevin to the house. Kevin arrived and threw his keys on the table.

"I quit," said Kevin.

"OK," replied Jack.

"Jack, I'm gonna quit!" shouted Kevin.

"I heard what you said," said Jack.

Jack asked Kevin to listen to a song by country singer Red Steagall, "Riding for the Brand," before he made his final decision.

Remember it was you
Who asked for the job,
So don't bitch when you ride for this brand.
Mr. Waggoner don't hold with complainers,
He'll fire one before he can quit.
So if you don't like your outfit,
Then head down the trail,
Find a hoss that your saddle will fit.
But if you get up early
And catch your own bronc,

Wrestling the World

Show the boss that you're makin' a hand;
Mr. Waggoner'll be there
To cover your bets
As long as you ride for his brand.

Kevin gave it some thought and decided to stay on. Jack was relieved.

Jack knew the bond situation was bad, but he wasn't sure what to do next. He reached out to a friend who told him he hadn't been damaged yet, he needed to let things unfold. Jack waited, not patiently.

The events that transpired almost cost Jack everything he'd ever worked for; the ranch, his good name and all his assets.

The development of 1,000 luxury homes depended on the county redrawing the urban limit line. The needed change was rejected. The homes were never built, and the revenue bonds proved worthless.

Unbeknownst to Jack, Pierce filed for bankruptcy in April 2001. The ranch had defaulted on the repayment of the bonds. By July 2002, Roddy Ranch filed for bankruptcy. For the next six months, Jack and Donna retreated in embarrassment from public life. They felt responsible for the investors' losses. Finally, after being cleared of any wrongdoing by the FBI, Jack called the press. He invited reporters out to the ranch to "clear the air."

The reporters showed up and Jack explained the Roddy Ranch bond measure was just a small part of Fitzgerald's scheming. Pacific Genesis had sold over $300 million dollars of the unsecured revenue bonds since 1995, he told them. He answered questions for hours; he had nothing to hide, he told them. As Jack recalled, "The public knew then that there was nobody madder than me about all this fraud."

The Antioch Ledger Dispatch ran the story the next day, along with this cartoon.

Illustration by Annette Balesteri
Special to the Ledger Dispatch

Wrestling the World

In 2005, Jack sued Pierce, alleging he "secretly diverted for 'his personal benefit' millions of dollars intended for the Roddy Ranch Golf Course and housing development. Roddy also alleged Pierce used $80,000 in funds earmarked for Roddy Ranch for another development," as reported in The Morgan Hills Times on Dec. 12, 2005.

"I've always tried to help Jack and look out for Jack's interests," Pierce told the Contra Costa Times. "If it hadn't been for me, he would have lost the ranch to foreclosure years ago."

"Jack is a trusting individual and he assumes that people will treat him the same way he treats people, honestly and fairly," Jack's attorney, Clem Glynn told the Hollister Free Lance on February 12, 2005. "Instead, the Pierces cost him a great deal of money, heartache and time. He believed they were trustworthy, and they were not."

The Hollister Free Lance reported that Pierce claimed he too had been duped by Fitzgerald and Pacific Genesis, and he had taken no money from the Roddy Ranch deal.

Pierce and his wife filed for bankruptcy in January 2010, the Dispatch reported later that month, owing more than $71 million in another failed development near Gilroy.

David Fitzgerald, targeted by state and federal authorities, was barred from acting as a broker for five years. Lawyers said he "disappeared," leaving bondholders holding the bag.

The consequences of the fraud, and his dealings with Pierce and Fitzgerald, would continue to dog Jack.

The ultimate price would be high.

Katie Cooney

Aerial view of Roddy Ranch Golf Course in Brentwood, CA.

Chapter 17

'He lived to beat me, and I lived to beat him.'

As the Scotswoman episode at Sierra Ranch made clear, Jack was always willing and eager to pursue a laugh. He'd learned how to play pranks from his mentor, Charlie Maggini, and his father in the banshee-tree episode in Ireland. He'd worked to refine the art throughout his youth.

His sense of mischief continued when he and golf pro Kevin Fitzgerald worked together at Roddy Ranch Golf Course. Jack trusted Kevin like a son, until he didn't. He was Jack's "right hand guy". Kevin had discovered the Genesis bond scheme and revealed it to Jack. The pair began a campaign to out-prank each other.

Jack started to play pranks on Kevin shortly after he'd arrived in 1998. Kevin quickly learned the value of reciprocating. Over the next 17 years, Jack and Kevin carried on a private war.

"He lived to beat me and I lived to beat him. I'm pretty good at pulling jokes," Jack recalled in a 2014 interview.

The friendship between Kevin and Jack only deepened over the years. Jack introduced Kevin to his future wife, a dear friend's daughter. They married and had children. The family moved into a house on the ranch to be closer to work and the Roddys. Over the years, Jack and Donna treated the family like their own. They included them in holidays, birthdays and festivities. The Roddy's committed to paying for the children's college education, Kevin the executor and beneficiary in their will.

A month before the golf course opened, Jack enjoyed having friends over to play a round. Jeff Severson invited his well-known Hollywood actress girlfriend from Los Angeles to join them.

"Is this your golf course?" the attractive actress asked Jack.

"Yeah, this is my private golf course. I made some money in the stock market and stuff," Jack said. "So, I built this golf course and I love it. I just invite a few of my friends to come up and play once in a while."

"Is this whole ranch yours?" she asked.

"Yeah, I bought the ranch a couple of years back," he said. "I don't know much about horses, but that's why Severson comes up every year, to teach me how to rope and how to do these cowboy things. I've never really spent much time around horses," Jack said.

After golfing, they drove to the ranch for dinner and drinks.

She walked into the trophy room and her mouth dropped, there were wall-to-wall rodeo trophies, saddles, buckles and photographs of Jack's winning moments.

"You're the lying-est son of a bitch!" she accused him.

They had a laugh.

The next night, football coach Bill Meyers flew in from Texas. They enjoyed a few drinks poolside and retold stories. The air was heavy, and the summer sun was about to set. Severson turned and asked, "Hey Jack, what time are they coming out?" Jack replied, "Probably another half-hour."

Kevin heard the exchange and his interest was aroused.

"Hey what are you guys talking about? What's coming out?" asked Kevin.

"Snipe," Jack replied.

Wrestling the World

Kevin enjoyed hunting, but he'd never heard of a snipe and doubted its existence. He snorted and declared there's no animal called a snipe. Jack shook his head in disappointment and explained in a fatherly way what a snipe was. Jack extended his hands to demonstrate the size of a snipe. It was about the size of two soccer balls and couldn't fly. They lived in the hills around the ranch and came out at night. You could tell when they were close because they made a distinctive clicking noise.

As Jack spoke, the actress became intrigued and hung on every word. She decided she wanted to see a snipe too.

Jack explained if they really wanted to see the snipe, it required the correct equipment; a garbage bag and a metal pie tin, one for each hand to hear the clucking of the snipe. Jack told them from his experience, "Hold the garbage bag and pie pan up so you can hear the clicking."

Kevin and the actress drove to the grassy pasture just in sight of the back patio. They made their way into the field with garbage bag and pie tin in hand.

The group at the house watched Kevin and the actress zero in on the snipe. Balancing the garbage bags and pie tins just above their heads they listened for the clicking.

When the pair moved to the right, Jack would holler across the pasture, "No the other way, they're going the other way, go left, go left!"

For 20 minutes, the shining pie pans reflected the warm glow of the setting sun as the two ran around in the pasture trying to find the snipe. Jack kept hollering, directing them: "Right there, I see them! Go to your right! Go to your right! No! Now left!"

After an hour of searching, the two realized: They'd been had. When they arrived back, empty-handed, the friends exploded in laughter.

The next day, Kevin called his dad back in New York and asked him if he knew what a snipe was. Mr. Fitzpatrick laughed and said, "You dummy. You don't know what a snipe is?"

And the pranks continued.

The hills surrounding Roddy Ranch were full of wild pigs. Jack invited Kevin on a pig hunt. "Hey, New York, are you tough enough to go shoot those wild pigs with me? asked Jack.

They walked out to the sixth hole, loaded the guns and cut across the golf course and broke into a run up the hill. Jack was in top shape after recently starting a running regimen. When Jack reached the hilltop, he looked back and saw "a red-faced Irishman."

They returned, empty-handed, to the sixth hole. Jack offered Kevin a friendly wager.

"You're not in too good of shape, New York."

"I can outrun you!" Kevin replied.

"I bet you a $100 you can't outrun me to the clubhouse."

"You're on!"

The two took off. The clubhouse was a good 150 yards from the sixth hole. Jack was in the lead; this was an easy win.

Jack heard Kevin screaming, "I'm tying up! Tying up!" Jack turned, and Kevin was nowhere in sight. He jogged a little further, turned again to scan the fairway. Still no Kevin.

Jack went back and found him writhing and screaming in pain.

Fear knifed through Jack. Kevin was in agony because of his silly bet. Jack raced to him, knelt and asked if he was OK.

Kevin sprang to life and bolted toward the clubhouse. He never looked back and reached the clubhouse gasping for air. Kevin won.

Wrestling the World

Jack made good on the bet. Kevin was one up on Jack.

Days after the race to the clubhouse, the staff gathered for their weekly all-hands meeting. Jack decided this was the place to challenge Kevin to another race. This time the wager was $500.

In front of the staff Jack said, "I'm going to bet you $500 that I can run you from the first tee-box to the green." Kevin laughed and wholeheartedly agreed. This was easy.

The race took place during a tournament. Jack explained the bet to the tournament director, and he agreed to judge. He held $500 from each competitor.

Jack and Kevin lined up at the starting point as the staff gathered to watch.

"GO!" the director shouted.

Kevin shot across the starting line and headed for the first tee-box. Jack, in his cowboy boots and hat, skipped across the green like a butterfly in spring. The staff wondered if he'd lost his mind; Kevin was sure to win.

Kevin reached the first tee box and started his dash back. The staff cheered him on. They felt a little sorry for Jack, who appeared so out of shape.

"Give me my money!" shouted Kevin passing the finish line.

"Oh no, no, no," said the tournament director.

"Give me the money!" Kevin demanded.

Jack returned and said to Kevin, "I told you I'd run you from the first green to the first tee-box and back. I didn't say I'd outrun you. You ran from the first green to the tee-box and back, just like I bet you would."

Jack turned to the tournament director and said, "Give me my money."

Jack won the bet using his words, not his legs.

Katie Cooney

One day at the clubhouse, Jack was chatting with golfers, when he saw Kevin with a clipboard looking intent and busy. Jack asked him what he was doing. Kevin said he was taking inventory in the Pro Shop; he suspected merchandise was being stolen.

Jack scanned the shop and told Kevin he could "steal the place blind." He explained to Kevin that after 40 years in the bar business it wasn't a matter of "if" people stole from you; it was rather "how much." Jack bet Kevin he could steal $500 worth of merchandise in a week, "right under your nose," and not get caught. They shook on it.

As Jack left the Pro Shop, he wished everyone a good day and slipped a sleeve of golf balls up his shirt sleeve.

Jack started a list, "Items stolen from the Pro Shop."

The columns included the date, item and cost:

Item #1 - Friday; Sleeve of golf balls; $9.95.

Jack returned to the clubhouse. Jack approached Kevin and halfway through the conversation another employee interrupted. As the employee told Kevin the problem with a golfer, Jack lifted a pair of leather gloves and another sleeve of balls.

Jack told Kevin to take care of the problem.

Item #2 - Friday; Leather golf gloves; $39.95.

Item #3 - Friday; Sleeve of golf balls; $9.95.

The following day it was cold. Jack put on a heavy jacket and headed to the clubhouse. He greeted the staff and took off his coat.

He left wearing a designer golf jacket and popped a Roddy Ranch baseball cap on his head to boot.

Item #4 - Saturday; Golf Jacket; $169.95.

Wrestling the World

Item #5 - Saturday; Roddy Ranch Golf Cap; $12.95.

On Monday, Jack met Kevin in his office and noticed a brand-new pair of top-end golf shoes.

Jack and Kevin chatted, when again they were interrupted by an employee who had a problem with a reservation. The distraction provided the opportunity to swipe the black and white shoes. Again, Jack told Kevin to attend to the issue, they'd talk later.

Item #6. Monday; Kevin's new golf shoes; $225.00.

The next morning, the staff were lined up in a single file on the green. Kevin was shouting, demanding to know who'd stolen his new black and white golf shoes.

Jack told Kevin he'd stolen the shoes, along with $500 in other merchandise.

Kevin installed cameras to monitor theft. Jack believed he'd taught Kevin a valuable lesson. And had pulled another one on him.

Jeff Severson decided to play a joke on Jack. He called Kevin and explained it. He asked Kevin to take out an ad in the Antioch Ledger Dispatch and advertise an event at Roddy Ranch Golf Course. The event offered free golf balls, golf clubs, T-shirts, hats and a free barbecue.

Kevin called Jack and warned him about the prank. Jack thought it was a fabulous idea and decided to turn it back on Severson. Jack called the Long Beach newspaper where Severson lived.

It was the week of the Grand Prix in Long Beach. Three hundred thousand fans and celebrities were expected. Jack placed the ad in the Sports section: Long Beach's own Super Bowl Champion and Cal State Long Beach Athletic Hall of Famer Jeff Severson will host an event at this year's Grand Prix. Free leather footballs, jerseys and 8x10 autographed photos. In addition, a free wine tasting. All donations benefit the Jeff Severson Snipe Fund. At the bottom of the ad it listed Severson's cell number for more information.

On the Grand Prix opening day, Severson's cell phone woke him. He let it go to voicemail. The phone never stopped ringing. He finally answered. The caller wanted more information about the free Severson event and the wine tasting. Severson got a newspaper and saw the ad in the sports section. His girlfriend laughed, "I thought you were going to screw him. Looks like he got you first."

Jack and Kevin called Severson.

"Is this Severson?" asked Kevin.

"Yes," Jeff answered.

"I watched you in both of those Super Bowls and you couldn't play football worth a damn. And you can stick that 8x10 photograph up where the sun don't shine!" laughed Jack.

In 1993, Jack felt achy and not quite himself. He knew something was off. His doctor tested his blood and the results shocked them both. Jack had a brain tumor. He needed brain surgery. At that time, it consisted of cutting the top part of the skull, pulling it back and going after the tumor. Patients often lost their sight or smell.

Dr. Robert Jampus, a Stanford brain surgeon and friend, was also a Rancheros Vistadores member. Jack had nicknamed him "Super Quack," and trusted him completely.

At Stanford, a scan showed a tumor the size of a plum—the largest the surgeon had seen, he said. It was a miracle the tumor hadn't already killed him, doctors told Jack; one good bulldogging knock on the front of the head could have killed him.

Before the Monday surgery, the anesthesiologist visited. He told Jack he'd give him a Valium before surgery, then knock him out. Jack told him he was a "little hard to numb and knock out." The doctor said he could knock him out in four seconds. "I bet you a drink you can't knock me out in four seconds," Jack challenged him.

Monday morning, they rolled Jack into the surgical theater. "You remember our bet?" he confirmed with the anesthesiologist. "Look at the clock," the doctor told him. "The minute I give you the injection, start counting to four," the doctor said. Jack got to three.

A young surgeon extracted the tumor through Jack's nasal cavity instead of his skull.

After, the surgery Jack woke up and declared, "You got me!"

Wednesday morning, Jack decided to get cleaned up. He heard his friend Jampus outside the bathroom door, shouting, "Roddy! Get your ass out here!"

"Super Quack, what's the matter with you?" Jack asked.

"You're getting out of this hospital! The nurses called my office and said they found a wastepaper basket full of cocktail mixes. I heard you had a party after your brain surgery!"

Friends had shown up and snuck in a supply of liquor, ice and mixers into Jack's room.

"Well, we had a good time," laughed Jack.

Jampus laughed too. Jack made an amazing recovery and was released the next day.

When word got out Jack had undergone brain surgery, flowers flooded the hospital, but he'd already gone. Dr. Jampus asked what he wanted them to do with all the flowers. Jack laughed and said, "Tell those guys to send me rodeo entrance fees!"

A week after being diagnosed with a dangerous brain tumor, four days after surgery, Jack was back rodeoing in the arena.

Between 1956 and 2017, Cal Poly rodeo teams had earned 44 national titles and cemented its standing as one of the most successful programs in the National Intercollegiate Rodeo Association.

In the 1990s, the rodeo team was under threat. The rodeo arena was bulldozed for a soccer field. If the rodeo program was to survive, they needed $100,000 in donations to build an arena.

Mike Barr, Director of Advancement for the College of Agriculture, and Joseph Jen, Dean of Agriculture, visited Jack in the summer of 2000. They needed his help to save the rodeo program. He'd handle it, Jack told them. The Roddy's would host a fundraiser at Roddy Ranch to support "Cal Poly's great rodeo tradition."

"When I went to Poly, I really didn't go there to learn as much as I did to rodeo, but it's the carrot that got me there. After I did go there, I did learn. And a lot of people in life got to be my bankers, my partners and opened many doors for me to get what I have today. So, I have to attribute that to Cal Poly. And rodeo's the carrot that got me there," Jack said in a 2014 interview.

"The Greatest Gathering of Cal Poly Rodeo Alumni and Friends Ever!" was held in September 2000. Over 1,300 joined in. The first day featured a team-roping competition, wine tasting and an auction, followed by a barbecue dinner, live music and dancing. The next day was spent golfing at the newly opened Roddy Ranch Golf Course.

Phoebe Hearst and Jack Cooke donated seven of the 12 horses auctioned the first day. Pat and Monty Roberts, Dave Wood, John W. Lacey and Jack Sparrowk also donated horses. The Cookes bought the horses they donated. That auction raised $90,000.

The event raised a quarter-million dollars, one of the largest off-campus fundraising events in Cal Poly history.

The new arena was built and the surplus funds of $150,000 were used for scholarships.

Rodeo continued at Cal Poly.

Chapter 18

*'I'm proud of what I was, what I did. Everyone still
loves a cowboy, so treat it with respect.'*

The Roddys hosted dozens of charitable events at the ranch. The annual Cal Poly State University NorCal Golf Tournament raised scholarship funds for underprivileged students. The California Cattlemen's Association and other local non-profits used the ranch to entertain and receive donations.

The Walnut Creek Rotary Club brought international students from UC Berkeley to visit the ranch and experience ranch life. The students came from around the world—Japan, Egypt, as far away as Uganda. The students all knew the most famous American cowboy, John Wayne. Jack told them the history of cowboys in America and the role Spanish and Mexican vaqueros played in establishing and enriching the American West.

Jack's trophy room filled them with excitement. Cameras snapped and photos showed Jack with his winning saddles, buckles and trophies. The students called him "John Wayne." Jack was awarded the Rotary International Paul Harris Award for his volunteer work with the international students and for mentoring young people in Antioch.

"Mentoring young people makes me feel good. I want to pass on what I've learned and keep the tradition alive," Jack said during a July 2018 interview. Jack had taught Stan "The Man" Holek to wrestle steers years before in San Jose and loved the experience. He mentored rodeo champs John Jones, Jr., Bob Marshal, Tommy Ferguson, Pat McCarthy, Aaron Russell and Chris Lybbert.

Jack volunteered to speak about ranch life and perform a roping demonstration for a crowd of more than 500 local Boy Scouts at the fairgrounds. He impressed the boys with his roping, then told them where their food came from.

"You know, I want to tell you about one thing," he said. "Your meat is not raised at McDonald's. It comes from a ranch. Ranchers take care of cattle. We raise them. And we protect the animal. Your milk doesn't come out of a carton. It comes from a cow.

"Now, I've got a ranch with beef cattle. And these cattle are big and strong. And, on my ranch, a certain percentage of steer will get either bit by a rattlesnake, step in a squirrel hole or get pneumonia. They don't understand English. And the only one that can save them is me. And with all our technology today, they'll never replace the horse and the cowboy and the rope. Because on my ranch, I do stuff not much different from what they did 150 years ago.

Now, on my ranch, if a steer is sick, I rope them, which I'm good at and my wife Donna is too. We'll heel them (rope their hind feet to hold them still), give them a shot and then they heal over the next several days," explained Jack.

Jack asked if there were any questions. Arms flew into the air. One boy asked if it hurt the animals when he roped them. Then another boy asked about hurting the animals. This gave Jack pause. Years earlier, Scouts would ask him if he knew such famous cowboys as fictional cowboy hero Hopalong Cassidy, John Wayne or Roy Rogers. They'd ask his horse's name and if he'd ever been bucked off. But not today, and that irritated Jack. Jack invited one Scout from each troop and their troop leaders out to the ranch, to show them how he and Donna took care of the cattle.

That spring, the Scouts and their leaders arrived at the ranch. The boys filed into the covered arena to watch the Roddys tend to a steer.

Jack explained why they'll never replace a cowboy, horse and rope. He told the Scouts when the steers come in from Kona, Hawaii, they set them loose in the pasture to graze on fresh grass. If a cowboy sees a steer lying down in the morning and not grazing—"off his feed"—he knows the steer may have shipping fever or pneumonia; a machine can't do that.

Wrestling the World

Cowboys need to understand how a steer moves, grazes, behaves to care for them properly. When the steer is sick, cowboys need to rope the steer to assess their condition. A sick steer can't walk to the barn to be diagnosed. The nuances of that understanding come from years of experience and a love of the animals.

"Now guys, I've got this steer. I can handle him in the arena but imagine he's two miles away. He'll die. And I'm not going to let him die. Now, he doesn't speak English. I can't walk up and say, 'Come here,'" he told the Scouts.

Jack explained how an 850-pound Corriente Mexican steer was bitten by a rattlesnake in the pasture earlier in the year. Jack saw the steer with a swollen leg as he passed on horseback. A group of cowboys went out and roped the steer and attended to the snake bite in the pasture and saved its life.

Jack and Donna demonstrated how they'd doctored the snake-bitten steer. Jack built a loop, made his throw and caught the animal around the neck. Donna caught its hind legs, heeling it. They dallied up, wrapping the ropes around their saddle horns, edged their horses backward to take up the ropes' slack and stretched the animal until it was immobilized. A ground worker vaccinated the steer, they let the slack off their ropes and the steer kicked free and trotted away.

"Any questions?" asked Jack.

"Do it again!" the Scouts screamed.

Jack felt a deep satisfaction.

The Roddys loved educating young people. They thought about turning the ranch into an educational center where future generations could learn about the American West, cowboys and ranch life. That dream took shape years later.

In the summer of 2010, the Roddys hosted the California Cattlemen's Association fundraiser. The ranch filled with cowboys, cowgirls and horses.

Jack and Dr. Bert Johnson rode to the roping sign-in station by the arena, adjacent to the announcer's box. When Jack leaned over to sign in, his horse bucked straight up, launching him over the horse's head. He cartwheeled to the ground, landing on his side. Johnson "heard Jack's ribs go," he said.

Johnson shouted for someone to call an ambulance. A crowd gathered. Johnson knew Jack was badly hurt and Jack knew from the searing pain ripping through his chest he was in bad shape.

The medics loaded him into an ambulance and raced to the local clinic.

Diagnosed with six broken ribs, he coughed blood and held his chest in pain. A few hours later, the clinic released him.

Back at the ranch, Johnson suspected something more wrong than what the X-rays had revealed. Jack belonged in the hospital, he thought. The Johnson's returned home, but worried about Jack's condition.

Cattle were shipping that week. Donna had to manage alone as Jack lay in bed. She'd never seen him in such pain. After two days, she took him back to the hospital. She knew something was wrong.

Another set of X-rays revealed a punctured lung; he'd also broken a collarbone. Pneumonia set in. They induced a coma and rushed him to surgery. It took 200 stitches to close the wounded lung.

After three days in a coma Jack awoke but couldn't walk. He'd spend one month in the hospital recuperating and learning to walk again in physical therapy. The full recovery took six months.

In 2013, Jack traveled to Ireland to make the documentary, "Cowboys in Ireland." Friend and fellow horseman Chris Cox spearheaded the Double Diamond C production. Jack reunited with family at the farm in Ballaghaderreen, saw family in Dublin and attended a steeplechase.

Jack was old friends with Cox, a filmmaker, producer and horse trainer. Jack and Cox's father Gene, a bronc rider, attended Cal Poly together in the late '50s.

Wrestling the World

Cox hosts the Chris Cox Horsemanship television show on digital cable and satellite station RFD-TV which covers issues and concerns about rural America. The show also illustrates horsemanship techniques and teaches people how to interact with and train their horses.

In Dublin, they met Jack's cousin and her son in a downtown pub. They hadn't seen one another for 65 years. They reminisced about his visit in 1947. As the band played Irish songs and the crowd sang along, Jack felt moved by the moment. His father's childhood of struggle and his fight for success, made lasting impressions. Jack admired how the Irish had immigrated to the United States, worked hard, educated their children and instilled in them a desire to succeed. Jack attributes his drive, his "never give up" attitude and his sense of justice to his father.

They visited the family farm. Cousin James Junior greeted them on the 40-acre farm he manages, with its 20 beef cows and 20 dairy cows. Smiles, laughter and hugs were plentiful.

When Jack had visited as a boy, the children told him of a mysterious, holy well on the side of a hill called the Blessed Well. Legend said the water was cursed and would never boil. Two people who had tried to boil it had died shortly after the story went. Each August, locals trekked to the well with offerings and trinkets, left them and prayed for special intentions or blessings.

When Jack heard about the holy well, he ran straight to the house and found a jar. Returning, he'd scooped up a can full of the magic water and boiled it. When his grandmother found out, he got a Gaelic tongue lashing.

Jack and Jimmy visited the Reagan sister's old house, where John and Uncle Michael had pretended to be banshees. They recalled the story and the summer Jack visited. Great memories.

The trip to Ireland was emotional for Jack. Visiting the family farm brought back memories of his father and the pranks he had played. The trip highlighted the opportunities Jack had in his life; the education he received at Cal Poly, the championships he'd won, the bars he owned, the cattle business, the mentoring and charity work…and most importantly, the friends he made along the way.

Jack Roddy singing at a Cal Poly fundraiser held at Roddy Ranch.

Jack Roddy teaching children to rope.

From left, Monty and Pat Roberts with Donna and Jack Roddy at Roddy Ranch. Photo credit: Katie Cooney.

From left, Buddy Simons, Dr. Patrick Johnson, Jack Roddy, Chris Cox and Jeff Severson, at Ballaghaderreen Chapel, Ireland in 2013.

From left, Jack Roddy, Katie Cooney, Jeff Severson and Bill Meyers at a fundraiser held at Roddy Ranch, 2013.

Chapter 19

'He picked the worst guy in the world to get in a fight with.'

What appeared to be an almost father-son relationship between Jack and Kevin Fitzgerald would prove to be something far different—and costly.

In 2014, Jack offered Kevin the opportunity to lease the golf course, instead of continuing to contract with an outside management company. Kevin jumped at the opportunity. He formed Roddy Ranch Golf Management and took over both golf-course and club operations. Jack concentrated on running cattle.

Kevin was the driving force behind building a new clubhouse that offered better amenities to compete with other courses.

Jack had long been interested in solar power and the solar-farming industry. Solar panels seemed like a natural fit, with little to no impact on the land or wildlife. The Roddys decided to bet on Kevin to manage the solar panel project. They borrowed $800,000 from a bank to fund the project.

Beginning in 2012, California suffered a statewide drought for over four years. Roddy Ranch Golf Course joined the "Brown is the New Green" campaign to conserve water. In 2016, brown spots appeared on the greens due to water rationing, Kevin claimed, but he assured golfers everything was fine with the business.

The drought dragged on as the new clubhouse readied to open, and the solar panels were delivered.

The new clubhouse and bar opened in January 2016. It was an instant success, with the live music, a festive atmosphere and the chance to meet and hear a story from local cowboy and celebrity Jack Roddy.

A few months later, Kevin asked Jack if he thought they might sell their golf course. Jack was taken aback; he'd assumed enough money was coming in to cover expenses. But Kevin said he couldn't pay the increasing water costs.

Jack called the local water department. He learned the golf course had failed to pay its bills for several months. He knew something was off and asked Kevin to the ranch. Jack called the local water department. He learned the golf course had failed to pay its bills for several months. He knew something was off and asked Kevin to the ranch. What transpired shattered the relationship they'd shared for 17 years. Kevin confessed he'd been stealing from Jack. He'd tried to cover his embezzling, but admitted he could no longer keep up the deception, Jack recalled frankly.

He told Jack he'd schemed with a contractor to steal $200,000 from the $800,000 solar project loan. Prosecutors alleged he'd used some of the money to cover lease payments and other costs at the golf course and taken the rest for himself.

Jack called the district attorney's office. Then he asked a consulting firm to operate the golf course and assess its financial viability. Touchstone Golf advised him to shut it all down.

Roddy Ranch Golf Course announced it would close on August 11, 2016 and join the growing list of golf courses closing due to the increased cost of water.
In April 2017, Kevin Fitzgerald was a fugitive. The notice was posted on the Northern California "Most Wanted" website.
East Bay Times reporter Nate Gartrell wrote on April 18, 2017, "Authorities say Fitzgerald and (the contractor) concocted a series of schemes which netted them hundreds of thousands of dollars. Some of the money Fitzgerald spent trying to salvage the golf club, which went under in August."

"When they tried—and failed—to get an additional $93,000 loan, Fitzgerald allegedly broke several of the club's solar panels and filed a fraudulent police report saying the property had been vandalized."

"He also told police, falsely, that more than 300 panels had been stolen, then filed fraudulent insurance reports seeking a settlement. It worked; he was given $267,000, spent some of it on the business and split about $100,000 with (the contractor), according to authorities."

Kevin surrendered on charges of "grand theft, diverting construction funds, theft from an elder or dependent, attempted grand theft, filing a false police report, and insurance fraud," the East Bay Times reported April 18, 2017.

"This is not to be bragging, but I've never lost a fight in my life, including fights with my fists," Jack stated. "I've never gotten into a fight looking for it, I've always backed up. But when it came my way, including the federal government, including this county on a thing called the urban limit line, including the federal government, the Dairy Diversion program, I didn't back down. I always told Kevin, if you're gonna fight me you'd better get to high ground, because I'm gonna try to get higher than you. And if you've got a cap gun, I'll have cannon. That's not bragging, it's just understanding that life is a battle. And if that's what it takes, that's what I'm gonna do. I don't like losing. Losing is not in my vocabulary," Jack declared in a 2016 interview.

Kevin solicited loans from golfers, stating Jack was backing the loans. Kevin also made it clear Jack didn't want to be bothered with the finances, so best not to talk to him about it.

Kevin "pleaded guilty to charges of fraud and theft after stealing over $300,000 from owner Jack Roddy over the course of two years," The Press - Brentwood, Discovery Bay, Oakley, Antioch reported December 14, 2017.

Fitzgerald was sentenced to six years in prison.

The Roddy's chosen son, the executor of their estate who stood to inherit 85 percent of their holdings, was headed for prison.

Jack felt bad for those who'd been taken in by Kevin's schemes. Through the tumultuous year there was a silver lining: His legacy of preserving the ranch and land for future generations. That legacy would come to pass, but not as Jack had imagined it. The land would be preserved, but not as a cattle ranch.

From left, Jack Roddy, Monty Roberts, Chris Cox and Jeff Severson at the new Roddy Ranch Golf Course Clubhouse in 2016. Photo credit: Katie Cooney

Wrestling the World

From left, Jeff Severson, Kevin Fitzpatrick, Bill Meyers, Chris Cox, Jack Roddy, Jerry Fletcher and Buddy Simons at the newly reopened Roddy Ranch Golf Course Clubhouse, 2016. Photo credit: Katie Cooney.

From left, Monty Roberts, Chris Cox, Pal Roberts and Jack Roddy at the new Roddy Ranch Golf Course Clubhouse, 2016. Photo credit: Katie Cooney.

1994, Champion Team Roper No. California Championship buckle.

1993, Prescott Gold Card World's Oldest Rodeo buckle.

Chapter 20

'I've lived the dream of being a cowboy.'

The Roddys continue to run their cattle business and raise quarter horses. In the last decade, they've pastured 600 to 1,000 Hawaiian steers. Although the Hawaiian Islands have acres of green pastures, the nutrients in the grass are diluted by constant rain. The cattle can't fatten on the grass and disease and pests keep Hawaii from growing feed corn. So, ranchers ship cattle to California to eat grass and grain and fatten up.

Cattle arrive from November to January, when the grass comes up strong and green in the pastures and ranges. Steers graze until the grass dries in mid-May to early June. Cattlemen load and ship their cattle to Colorado or Texas, where corn is cheaper. As Jack says, "It's cheaper to send the cattle to the grain, than the grain to the cattle." They're fed corn for 90 days and in the end, 90 percent is Choice beef.

Ironically, the beef is then shipped back to Hawaii, where Choice beef is preferred at resorts. The Hawaiian cattle market is more profitable than the historically unstable mainland market.

Running a cattle ranch in the middle of Brentwood, a growing East Bay suburb, is no easy task. People want to hunt the land, which the Roddys don't allow. People drive through fences and steers get loose and can cause accidents on the increasingly busy roads, which can lead to litigation. Neighbors worry about fires, so the Roddys graze areas with an eye toward protecting surrounding neighborhoods.

In a 2016 interview, Jack said they'd continue to run the business because "that's what my wife and I enjoy. That's what we are good at. We know what we're doing around here. We've got neighbors to protect. So, we've been here a long time and people respect us and we respect the ranch. I want it respected…If we were smart, we'd say the heck with it; let somebody else do it. But that's our life and that's what we've got to do."

In 2016, Jack received the Ben Johnson Memorial Award. Ben Johnson, rodeo champion, stuntman and Academy Award winner, was born in 1918. Johnson took a break from acting to compete in team roping. He was inducted into the ProRodeo Hall of Fame in 1973. He was prouder of his championship than anything else he'd ever done according to his ProRodeo Hall of Fame entry. He died of a heart attack in 1996.

Jack, Gordon Davis and Cecil Jones contributed to creating the Ben Johnson Memorial Award. The National Cowboy Museum states: The "Ben Johnson Memorial Award acknowledges a living individual who has been involved in the rodeo industry for a number of years and has contributed to the growth and betterment of pro-rodeo. Involvement with youth and/or community activities also is a prerequisite for the honor." The recipient is a person who's created a positive image for the sport of rodeo and the Western lifestyle.

In October 2016, Jack was awarded the Ben Johnson award at the Rodeo Historical Society banquet. Johnson was the epitome of what a cowboy should be, Jack said, and he was honored to join the ranks of Johnson and other rodeo champions, his friends and mentors.

Jumping ahead to 2017, Jack also was honored by the San Jose Sports Authority. On November 9, it inducted five new members into its Hall of Fame. Ken Caminiti, baseball all-star, Gold Glove Winner and 1996 National League MVP; Dwight Clark, San Francisco 49er wide receiver and Super Bowl winner; Mark Marquess, All American player/Gold Medal and NCAA championship coach; Danielle Slaton, national champion soccer player and Olympic medalist; and Jack Roddy, Rodeo Hall of Famer, collegiate and professional steer wrestling champion.

Each inductee was recognized with a bronze plaque on the concourse at SAP Center in San Jose. The San Jose Hall of Fame also includes Olympic skaters Kristi Yamaguchi & Peggy Fleming, Olympic runner John Carlos and World Cup soccer winner Brandi Chastain.

"Now 80, Roddy's dark hair has gone white, but he still cuts a towering figure topped with a white cowboy hat," San Jose Mercury News reporter Sal Pizarro, wrote at the time. "(The number of people in the audience wearing cowboy hats and boots—all Roddy fans and friends—was surely a record for the event.)"

In June of 2013, Jack spoke to the partners of Roddy Ranch Group LLC about selling their 1,990 acres to the East Bay Regional Parks District instead of pursuing any future housing development on the land. The partners agreed that selling and preserving the land was best.

That June, the park district bought the land, which included Deer Valley, in partnership with the East Contra Costa County Habitat Conservancy. Funding came from a bond measure, the Gordon and Betty Moore Foundation and the California Wildlife Conservancy Board.

"We're going to sell the ranch to the park. I'm not going to develop the land. When I leave this earth, I want to leave it better than when I found it," said Jack in a 2013 interview.

Jack and Donna retained ownership of their 40-acre ranch, two other parcels of land totaling 240 acres and Roddy Ranch Golf Course.

The acquisition was a once-in-a-lifetime opportunity for the park district to expand its holdings and enlarge an existing trail system at the base of Mount Diablo. Jack's land was sandwiched between two regional state parks. With the purchase, Deer Valley would connect one vast contiguous protected corridor below Mount Diablo.

"This is a significant conservation victory for the East Bay," said district General Manager Robert Doyle in The Press Brentwood Discovery Bay Oakley and Antioch, August 9, 2014. "The combined acquisitions preserve a huge and beautiful area of open space with a rich local history."

Mayor Wade Harper was delighted with the preservation, as were many Antioch residents. With the Roddy Ranch land, the new Deer Valley Regional Park was developed. It connects Black Diamond Mines Regional Park and Marsh Creek State Park.

The land hosts a menagerie of indigenous California wildlife: Red-legged frogs, tiger salamanders, the San Joaquin pocket mouse, American badger and burrowing owl, mule deer, coyote, and red-tailed and red-shouldered hawks inhabit the golden, rolling hills. Special-status species also have been seen there, including the San Joaquin kit fox, Alameda whipsnake, golden eagles, northern harriers and several species of bats.

After the Roddys signed the park deal, Jack took flak from developers who told him he'd sold too cheaply. But Jack told them he didn't live for money; preserving the land was more important to him. Kids won't learn anything, he told them, from seeing a swarm of bulldozers carving lots from the land for luxury houses.

Escrow closed a year later; the land was officially the park districts. Any chance of developing the land was quashed.

Ironically, the Earth First! organization and Unabomber Ted Kaczynski probably would have approved of conserving the land. And had Jack been hurt back in the 1990s, when his name was on terrorists' hit list, luxury homes in private neighborhoods might have covered the California hillsides and pasture lands where Natives had lived free and vaqueros once ran cattle and horses. Instead, it's preserved for generations to come and for the ghosts of those who've gone before.

In 2015, Jack was mending fence when Robert Doyle approached. He told Jack that interested donors wanted to turn his home ranch into an educational center bearing his name. The center would focus on agriculture, the American West and ranching life. Jack listened and declined Doyle's offer.

But the conversation stuck with him. He wondered what would happen to the ranch after he and Donna were gone. Jack told Donna he liked the idea that it could be a museum and place where kids could come out and get a taste of ranching and the old days. They agreed the ranch would be an ideal educational center.

Jack called Doyle and said they were interested.

Wrestling the World

In 2018, after a long year, Jack and Donna decided to sell their 40-acre ranch and golf course to the park district, with the option to lease back the ranch and land for 10 years.

Doyle said the former golf course will serve as a picnic area with bike trails and the trailhead to Deer Valley park.

Roddy Ranch will be converted to an educational center focusing on agriculture, ranching and the American West, bearing the Roddy name.

Currently, the district also runs the Sidney Flat Visitor Center for mining history; Tilden Nature Area for farming and farm animals; Tilden Regional Park - Botanical Garden, for native plants; and Sunol Regional Wilderness for Native American history.

At the 2019 Cal Poly Rodeo, Jack was honored for his lifetime achievements. Historians noted, he is the only cowboy to place first in five events and taking second in a sixth at a single rodeo. He secured the record and the All-Around Cowboy title to boot at the 1959 Pendleton Rodeo.

Today, Jack and Donna quietly carry on the day-to-day life of ranchers and cattlemen around the American West, keeping up the ranch, tending the herd and watching over the land.

As Jack said: "That's our life and that's what we've got to do."

Jack and Donna Roddy. Photo credit: Katie Cooney.

2017 San Jose Hall of Fame Inductee Jack Roddy. Photo credit: Katie Cooney.

2017 San Jose Hall of Fame Inductee Jack Roddy.
Photo credit: Katie Cooney.

Jack Roddy at home, 2017. Photo credit: Katie Cooney.

Donna and Jack at Roddy Ranch.

Donna and Jack at Roddy Ranch.

Donna working on Roddy Ranch.

Jack Roddy Cowboy Champion Trophy Room.

1997, Cattlemans Roping World Champion buckle.

1985, Rancheros Vistadores, All Around Champion - One Man, One Horse buckle.

First Place Rodeo Wins

Jack secured first place in steer wrestling at the following rodeos; Albuquerque, New Mexico; Billings, Montana; Cheyenne, Wyoming; Cody, Wyoming; Fort Worth, Texas; Honolulu, Hawaii; Livingston, Montana; Pendleton, Oregon; Ponoka, Alberta; Red Bluff, California; Reno, Nevada; Santa Maria, California; Sidney, Iowa; Spokane, Washington; Swift Current, Canada; Tucson, Arizona; and Tulsa, Oklahoma. He secured first place in an NFR Go Around in Oklahoma City, Oklahoma. He placed first twice at the Cow Palace in San Francisco, California. He won first place three times at the Salinas Rodeo.

Unbeaten World Record
Five Firsts and Placed in All Six Events at
Pendleton, Oregon Rodeo in 1959

In 1959, Jack won five first place titles at the Pendleton, Oregon Rodeo. First in steer wrestling, bull riding, saddle bronc riding, bareback riding and ribbon roping. He placed second in calf roping. Sixty years later, he is the only cowboy to win five firsts and place in all events at a single rodeo. Jack is a true All-Around Champion!

Katie Cooney

1990, Cow Place Quarter Horse Dally Team Roping and Heading buckle.

2000, National Finals Shoot Out buckle.

Epilogue

On a cool, crisp September morning in 2009 I attended a branding at Kathy and Danny Torre's ranch in Milpitas, California. Cowboy friend David Elkins had told me three well-known punchers were attending: Jack Roddy, Dr. Bert Johnson and Jack Sparrowk. For half a day, I photographed them rounding up 150 steers in the frost-tipped pasture, then pushing them into weather-worn wood corrals. They roped, vaccinated, and branded the steers, one after another.

After the branding, we shared steak, potato salad, beans, and fried Rocky Mountain oysters on an old wooden-door picnic table.

I sat across from Jack and listened to his stories of cowboying and life. I was hooked. We began to chat and discovered commonalities: both Irish descents, Cal Poly grads, a mutual love of the West. I asked Jack if there was a book about his remarkable life. He said no, nobody would believe it. "I would," I replied.

And the journey began.

Katie Cooney

From top clockwise, left, Jack Roddy, Dr. Bert Johnson and Jack Sparrowk, 2008.
Photo credit: Katie Cooney.

Acknowledgements

I'd like to express a special thanks to Rick Alpers who invited me to photograph his family cattle branding in the San Jose foothills in 2007. That day reignited my love for the West.

A year later at another Alper's branding, I met cowboy David Elkins. He invited me to the branding where I met Jack Roddy. Thank you to both great cowboys who welcomed me into the rodeo family and gave me the priviledge to meet two-time World Rodeo Champion Jack Roddy and document the story of a lifetime.

Katie Cooney

Wrestling the World

Thank You's

Those who shared their time, stories and memories and to those who lent their support, I sincerely thank you.

Dr. Bert "Ropin' Doc" & Gretchen (late) Johnson, Karin and Cotton Rosser, Wendy and Wade Elkins, Kathy and Danny Torres, Joyce Viera, Laura and Troy Hansen, Bonnie and Lee Rosser, Shirlee and Rick Alpers, Donna and Lindsay Alpers, Jeff Severson, Bill Meyers, John Ramirez, Pat and Monty Roberts, Linda and Billy (late) Adair, Jim Capps, Debbie Roberts-Loucks, Jerry Fletcher, Stacey Stadtler, Max Knoll, Judy Deggeller, Tracey Colella, Robin Pledger, Lauren MacKenzie, Andy Gettens, Kathleen Matthews, Chris Wilcox, Lisa Lane, Katie Ritchey, Nassim Nouri, Karen Gutfreund, Gail Zappetini-Pearson, Rachel Barkin, Carol Nast, the Staebell Family, Mike Ichikawa, Barbara Tyler, Angelina Mertens, Marian Roddy Sharp, Heather Sharp, Peter Coe Verbica, Silvia Martin, Rich Amooi, Laura Sorvetti - Cal Poly Archives, Maryann and Mike Brickman and Linda Meyer at CSU Fort Collins.

Thank you to my editor John McNicholas.

And thank you to Donna Roddy for her hospitality, kindness and graciousness.

Thank you to my great-grandparents, grandparents and my Cooney farming family who worked and lived in the plains of Holton, Kansas.

Thank you to California Polytechnic State University (Cal Poly), San Luis Obispo, CA, where I learned the greatest lesson, "Learn by Doing." Thank you to Cal Poly President Jeff Armstrong for supporting the long tradition of rodeo at Cal Poly.

Thank you to the United States of America, who gave my Irish relatives a chance to achieve their American Dream.

Lastly, thank you to my devoted and ever supportive husband, Kamlapati Khalsa.

Made in the USA
Las Vegas, NV
13 March 2025

19533477R00177